AT HOME WITH THE HOMELESS

By the same author:

Rudolf Hess and Germany's Reluctant War, 1939–41, The Book Guild 2001

AT HOME WITH THE HOMELESS

*Life at a Northampton Hostel
for Homeless Youngsters*

Alfred Smith

Book Guild Publishing
Sussex, England

First published in Great Britain in 2005 by
The Book Guild Ltd
25 High Street
Lewes, East Sussex
BN7 2LU

Typesetting in Times by
Keyboard Services, Luton, Bedfordshire

Printed in Great Britain by
CPI Bath

A catalogue record for this book is available from the
British Library

ISBN 1 85776 970 8

This book is dedicated to the memory of my late wife Nancy, who taught me the meaning of the word compassion

'Home is that place to which you return when you are away.'

Annie Smith (circa 1935)

Contents

Foreword by Mary Kenny

I can hardly recommend this book highly enough. I think everyone who has any concern for young people growing up in a troubled environment should read it. Alfred Smith, a father of four and grandfather of more, is clearly a man who cares a great deal for what he calls 'the outer shell and inner self' of so many young people – he estimates that there are 100,000 who are homeless and in trouble in Britain today. He sees them not as statistics but as individuals, with their own unique identities and their particular emotional 'baggage': yet he sees, also, the common threads in their lives which have so often gone into the cocktail of homelessness, trouble with the authorities and despair.

The most invariable of those threads is the phenomenon of the 'broken home' – that is to say, the all-too-frequent situation where a parent abandons the family home, followed swiftly by the arrival of a step-parent or new partner to the remaining parent, followed more swiftly again by the ejection of the young male from the home, usually at an alarmingly early age.

A most poignant example of this is the story of Pip, who lived a contented life with his parents until he was about 12: he especially treasured the experience of going fishing with his dad during those childhood years. But quite suddenly, his father quit the family home to cohabit with another woman: Pip's mother then acquired a new partner from overseas, and Pip was marginalised and left to his own devices. Almost inevitably he drifted into a pattern of petty crime and sleeping rough – propelled, too by a deep sense of anger and resentment against the much-loved father who had walked out on him.

'Smithy' was able to help the lad – though these processes are often lengthy and require much patience – and there is, finally, a happy ending when Pip finds the love of a good woman. But it is obvious that such young males often need a firm but caring father-figure to help them through the turbulent years, and 'Smithy' has been able to provide that for such lost souls. Developing a skill or a gift is often the route to helping repair such lives. And even so, some young lives are unfortunately irreparable. There is a heart-breaking account of a rackety young woman who, by the age of 18, is incorrigibly sexually promiscuous (and in the process, extremely self-destructive): Smithy discovers that she has the natural gift of a truly outstanding singing voice. But alas, her life has already been too ruinous of her self-worth – she has the talent, but not the character, to use her remarkable gift.

A child expert once said that all a young person needs, in early life, is *one* person who believes in him, utterly, and is unconditionally attached. So many of the young people that Alfred Smith has encountered have simply never had the love, the cherishing, the consistent and continuing attachment of that one person. (Occasionally, a grandmother has emerged as that one person, and has saved the individual.) Alfred Smith's conclusion is that there has been a collapse of responsible parenting: the values purveyed by much of the popular media are that personal happiness comes before responsibilities. In too many cases he has seen, the parents' sexual needs seem to have greater priorities than their duties to their children: a trail of abandoned young people pay the price. There *is* something to be said for trying to keep a marriage together for the sake of the children – at least until the offspring have been guided protectively through the turbulent teenage years.

A supercilious intellectual once said to Alfred Smith, 'Haven't you got anything better to do with your time than look after life's losers?' This compelling book demonstrates that there is scarcely a better calling than caring for those young people who so desperately need the care and attention of a kindly, patient, helpful and responsible adult who operates with compassion, common sense and a real sense of values. Alfred Smith's account is both engaging in itself and important in terms of framing social policies in the future.

Mary Kenny
Journalist and author
March 2005

Preface by Rose Stewart

I was delighted when the author asked me to contribute to his splendid book. He said that it needed an introduction by someone who, in terms of their own experience, understood what goes on in the heart and mind of the homeless youngster.

And Smithy himself? Well, it was several weeks into my post as house manager at the Junction Road hostel before I knew who he was. I did not know his full name for several months. I heard talk about Smithy, and was told by various young men who lived at Junction Road that he was 'a posh bloke who takes us on trips and stuff' and that he was 'this old bloke who takes us for driving lessons'. I knew from my colleagues at head office that he had formed the Friends of Valerie Hanson House at Junction Road. When I met him he was all of the descriptions and much more. We quickly became a formidable team in our work with the young men at the house. The young people in our care thought they could be scheming and manipulative. That was their way of life, but we got it down to a fine art – in a positive way I hasten to add. There were no lengths to which we wouldn't go in our quest to enhance the lives of those young people.

'It's better to build a child than repair an adult.' I can't remember whose quote that was, but it was on a plaque I was given by the then chair of the Junction Road committee, which I hung on my office wall at the house. This was the work which we embarked on in Junction Road. We were attempting to repair young adults whose families for whatever reason had failed to build them as children. Anger, resentment, rejection, loss of self-esteem, an intense dislike of anyone in authority and a complete denial of their need for love were just some of the masks worn by these young people. Some came through the door like the proverbial angels with dirty faces. Others arrived with a ready-made tough exterior, determined that they were going to rule the roost. Each one was a damaged individual who quickly learnt to become part of the subculture that pervaded the hostel. For some it was an 'in with both feet, no holds barred' entry. For others it was a 'keep my head down and see what happens' approach. However, for all of them it was a matter of survival.

Lazy, dossers, yobbos, tramps, little criminals – just some of the descriptions I have heard about the young men who resided at the house. More apt descriptions would have been lonely, afraid, disadvantaged, deprived and neglected. How could a young person attend college or go to work when some of them only had the clothes they stood up in when they arrived. They were often escaping abuse in many forms. For lots of them a step-parent had joined the family and given the partner a choice, him or me. Sadly, it was the child who usually seemed to lose out. The last thing they wanted was to get into mainstream living. To them that was a place that had rejected them, a place where they couldn't have fitted in even if they had wanted to. They didn't have the 'cool' trainers, trendy clothes or pocket money that their peers in these establishments had. For them, to join this culture meant further rejection. Many of them were illiterate and had survived without anyone realising this was the case. How can you go for a job when you can't even read the application form, let alone fill it in? How can you go for an interview when you have no decent clothes to put on? All these were very real obstacles which faced a lot of the young people in our care.

The biggest single difficulty we faced was the question of trust. How on earth were we going to build bonds with these young men when they had been unable to build bonds with their own flesh and blood? It was often expressed to me in a variety of ways by the youngsters. 'You only do it 'cos you get paid.' 'It's your job to be nice to us.' It was going to be a long haul, as they constantly pushed the boundaries, let us down and messed up. Consistency, patience and equality usually won the day, but it was a long-term struggle, not in a namby-pamby style but in a realistic 'accept responsibility for the choices you make' way. If one of them did anything which upset other people, was dishonest or abused the trust we gave them, they faced the consequences of those actions.

One of the biggest tools we had for building self-esteem at the hostel was Smithy's driving lessons. Most of the youngsters had no form of identity. They became people in their own right when they got their provisional driving licence. Without a form of identity, you can't open a bank account or prove who you are. Suddenly, with a driving licence, you are a person. Nine o'clock on Sunday mornings was driving-lesson time for whoever's turn it was. One o'clock would have suited them better. However, part of growing up and accepting responsibility was to be on time and occasionally to fit in with other people's agendas. The world did not owe them a living. If you were not outside the house by ten past nine then you missed your lesson. As this was one of their most pleasurable pursuits, they quickly learnt to get up and be on time.

Gradually bonds were made. Loyalty became evident and they began to care for each other. 'Family' was being established. Not all of them made it. Some were too damaged and could not let their masks slip. A lot of them, though, learnt to trust again. They began to want to get back into mainstream living. They were encouraged to dream their dreams along with the rest of us. Each time a new person joined the group the process started again. This time, however, their peers were part of the healing and worked alongside staff to empower the new resident.

It has been five years since I worked at Junction Road and the bonds are still there. I still see some of the young people who were part of the house and so does Smithy. We are now part of their families, 'grandchildren' and all.

I finish with one thought: you get what you expect. If you expect nothing you get exactly that. Smithy and I expected the best; in the end we generally got the best from the young men. I like to think we always gave them our best. Read on and see what you think.

Rose Stewart[1]
April 2004

---

[1] Rose Stewart was house manager of the hostel at Junction Road and is currently assistant housing manager with Northampton YMCA, responsible for the smooth operation of three YMCA centres.

Introduction

Once upon a time a small boy was walking along the seashore with his bucket and spade. Suddenly, there came a great wave which tossed hundreds of shellfish onto the beach far beyond the water-line. The small boy, realising the plight of the stranded shellfish, started picking up one or two at a time, putting them in his bucket and taking them down to the water's edge to throw them back into the sea. An onlooker said to the small boy, 'You're not going to save many like that, you know,' to which the small boy replied, looking in his bucket, 'No, but I shall save these two shan't I?'

In modern Britain there are over 100,000 homeless young men between the ages of 16 and 18. They have abandoned, or been abandoned by, either or both of their natural parents or those others who have assumed responsibility for their welfare as they approach manhood. A few, far too few, like shellfish in the small boy's bucket, find through the compassion of others a safe haven and a protected return to orderly living. This is the story of one such safe haven and some of the youngsters who were nurtured there.

My connection with the Valerie Hanson House Hostel for homeless young men came through my association with the Northampton Kitchen. The kitchen was and is a voluntary organisation financially backed by Northampton Corporation. It offers succour to those unfortunate people afflicted by alcoholism, drug addiction, psychological disorders or in some cases an inability to cope with the problems of mainstream living. The kitchen is situated in basement premises in one of the less salubrious districts of the town and is frequented by many of its customers on an almost daily basis. There they enjoy, in reasonable comfort, a warmth of fellowship with their peers, and soup, sandwiches and tea supplied free of cost by a volunteer staff. One is tempted to take a jaundiced view of the local government involvement, which is perhaps prompted by the perceived need to keep the kitchen's customers off the streets of Northampton. Nevertheless, the accommodation and facilities provide a place of rest and refuge for those in need and torment. When I joined the kitchen as a volunteer in the early 1990s, it was dealing with 30–40 customers daily and perhaps double that number on Sundays, when a hot meal was served. This scale of operation had grown out of the original drop-in facility run by the local Catholic priests and had come about through the tireless efforts of a quite remarkable woman, Valerie Hanson, supported by an enthusiastic team of committed volunteers, all of whom she had personally recruited.

In recent years Valerie had noted a disquieting trend in the make-up of those using the kitchen. They included an increasing number of young men in their teens. They were obviously unemployed and almost certainly sleeping rough. It was clear that this younger element were worth more than the kitchen could offer. Their lives still lay ahead of them. Were there latent skills and qualities which could still be developed before it was too late? Given the right environment and some personal encouragement, perhaps a major rehabilitation exercise could be possible and windows of opportunity opened up for these young men. And so it was that Valerie, being the female equivalent of Action Man, was soon in cahoots with St Matthew's Housing Society, a prominent and well-reputed national concern specialising in the provision of accommodation for the homeless. They had not previously entered into the field of youth work, but to their credit they were prepared to back Valerie's enterprise. As a result, and in what seemed no time at all, the Lord Lieutenant of Northampton, John Lowther, was duly presiding over the opening ceremony of the Valerie Hanson House Hostel for homeless young men on the morning of Tuesday 15 July 1993.

My own involvement in the new enterprise was immediate. With Valerie's blessing, I inaugurated the Friends of Valerie Hanson House to raise funds to help oil the wheels generally at the hostel and assist with the costs of the welfare, education and training of the residents. That was my sole original intention but gradually, and with growing interest, I also became involved with the residents themselves. The experience thus gained over a near ten-year period was a revelation. I had been blessed with four children and nine grandchildren of my own and therefore thought myself to be no novice in dealing with teenagers, but what I found at the hostel was new territory. I, a typical middle-class grammar school-educated chartered accountant, found myself trying to cope with representatives of a teenage subculture of which I was totally ignorant. I soon found that this culture had its own rules, regulations, values and codes of behaviour, all of which were foreign to me. At first, I was shocked to learn that such strictures – rather than those which were bread and butter to me – should circumscribe a young person's life. But, gradually, as I learned more and explored more – particularly about the personal histories and backgrounds of the young lives in question – I began to understand why this alien culture was so attractive to these young men and even to respect it.

All the incidents, events and reported conversations as set out in the pages that follow are true to the best of my knowledge and belief. Some are taken from actual case histories with which I was personally involved. They are I think typical examples of the sort of work with which we were involved. The actual names of the young men are used where I have obtained their permission. In other cases the names have been changed so as to avoid needless embarrassment. The contents of the book reflect my own experience rather than the fruits of academic research. The conclusions reached and opinions given, particularly in Chapter Nine, are therefore strictly personal, based as they are on that experience.

My particular thanks are due to my long-serving secretary, Sue Coolman, who, armed with an appropriate magnifying glass, has succeeded in deciphering my microscopic handwriting and has not only produced a readable text, but has not been afraid to hoist the storm-warning cones when my views started to drift towards the extreme.

And last, but certainly not least, my thanks are due to those young men I have been privileged to know and, yes, from whom I have learnt much over the years. They have made me laugh and they have made me cry. Above all, they have earned my respect. I wish every single one of them the best of good fortune in the future as some sort of makeweight for what have in so many cases been the misfortunes of the past.

Alfred Smith
April 2004
Northampton

Chapter One

Early Days

'You will be let down thousands of times by these youngsters, but never never ever let them down because they have been let down enough already. Then over the long term they will begin to trust you and then they will not let you down. The door to their world will then be opened to you and you may enter.'

Rose Stewart (circa 1994)

The premises at 1 to 3 Junction Road in the Kingsley district of Northampton, which on conversion became the Valerie Hanson House Hostel for homeless young men, had an unusual history. Originally, the premises was home to a plant that manufactured mineral water. The building had distinguished itself during the Second World War when a small aircraft belly-flopped onto its roof. The plane had force-landed on the nearby racecourse on the Saturday afternoon but hadn't quite made it when taking off on the Sunday morning.

Mindful of this quirk of history, the architects and builders, prompted by an ever-present Valerie, did not spare themselves on the conversion, and St Matthew's Housing soon became aware of the size of their capital investment. Accommodation was provided for eight residents. Each was to have his own room and his own key. There was to be no dormitory sleeping. If self-esteem was to be enhanced then some degree of privacy was essential. The rooms were small but adequate, with fitted washbasins and cupboards and a necessary minimum of furniture. All the woodwork was polished

1

light oak, promoting the overall newness and cleanliness of the accommodation. Toilet and showering facilities, again on an individual basis, were plentiful, and there was one giant-sized bath for those wishing to luxuriate. Apart from these private quarters, there were also communal areas – a reception lobby, a dining area and a lounge, all modestly but comfortably furnished, with light oak again in prominence. Last but not least, attached to the dining area was a square-shaped and well-equipped kitchen and utility area. The kitchen would of course have the important task of looking after the needs of eight hungry young stomachs. And to ensure that our young men would be smartly turned out as well as well fed, the utility area sported a jumbo washing machine capable of handling all the laundry requirements. There was also what was called 'the quiet room'. It was the first mistake. This room was situated on the ground floor at the rear of the premises away from the communal areas and the residents' rooms. The theory was that any lad wishing to withdraw from the ever-present noise provided by residents' music, their chatter and sometimes boisterous behaviour, for the purpose of reading, studying or a similar activity, could do so by retiring to the quiet room earmarked for that purpose. The reality was that all residents seemed to thrive on noise and ran to embrace it rather than withdraw from it. And reading and studying were never very high on the list of resident priorities – at least not in early days. In any case, it was soon found that space was required to handle the hostel's paperwork and financial administration. The quiet room thus soon became the hostel office.

In addition to the accommodation provided for the lads, there were two separate flats subjoined to the main premises to house the hostel manager and his or her assistant. The manager's ground-floor flat was at the rear of the premises and was self-contained with its own entrance. It was also connected to the rear of the hostel by a locked door.[1] If not sumptuous, the flat was, like the residents' accommodation, more than adequate. It also had a special feature – the French doors from the lounge opened out into an attractive walled garden of manageable proportions. Given some peace in the hostel, there was the prospect of a few hours peace in the garden. Different managers reached different levels of attainment in this regard. The manager's

---

[1] When off duty, the manager would often display a notice on the door to that effect, sometimes adding the words 'So please sod off'.

assistant also had a self-contained flat with all facilities included en suite. Finished in the same light-oak style as the residents' rooms, it was situated on the first floor of the hostel itself. It was thus vulnerable to residents' noise and to residents requiring attention. Both were irksome to an occupant looking for a few hours peace while off duty. A locked door and an appropriate notice when off duty was found to be little deterrent. Eventually, this enhanced accommodation was made available by way of reward to whoever was the senior resident, and the post of assistant manager was abolished.

Such was the theatre in which our great adventure was to be performed. But what about the players – our first residents and the St Matthew's staff designated to play the leading roles of house manager and his assistant? But first of all, before the curtain went up, there were the rules of engagement as it were, to be considered. In the event, they presented a particular problem in those early days that was still with us years later. To qualify for residency at the hostel, St Matthew's Housing stipulated that our young men had to pass through three hoops: they had to be between the ages of 16 and 18; they had to be homeless; and they had to give an undertaking to take up gainful employment or embark upon a course of study or vocational training. The first two conditions presented no difficulty. Registry records proved the first and the lads produced their own evidence as to the second. In most cases their homelessness was confirmed by the agencies introducing the young men to us – the social services, the Probation Service, the Youth Offending Team, the police, etc. I was appalled when I learned some of the details. One of our earliest applicants had slept rough on Northampton Racecourse for the best part of a year. Another had slept for months in the cab of the miniature railway engine at Wicksteed Amusement Park, Kettering. Another had regularly sought shelter and sleeping accommodation in the cubicles of Northampton's public lavatories. Apparently, all these places of residence were deemed preferable to whatever went for life at home. But it was the third condition which was to become a recurrent problem, and it was caused in most cases by a single factor.

School attendances by our lads in the early days had been at best spasmodic and at worst non-existent.[2] Basic education standards

---

[2] In their 2000/2001 annual report, the Office for Standards in Education stated that over five million days of education were being lost each year through truancy and absences sanctioned by parents.

therefore tended to be very low. In a number of cases, the young men passing through our hands were hardly literate and occupational skills were next to nil. Because of this shortfall we soon found that it was often very difficult, or even impossible, to get our lads to take up courses of study or other training with other students. Sitting in class with others soon advertised the fact of their basic educational inadequacies.[3] This led to much embarrassment and personal humiliation.[4] This particular difficulty was further accentuated by the attitude of the lads themselves. In many cases 'earnings' had arisen from the fringes, or even the heart, of petty-criminal activity.[5] Gainful and regular employment supported where necessary by the social-security benefit system or academic study was an aspect of mainstream living that they had rejected and which had rejected them. Residents might therefore readily sign up with the intention of finding gainful employment or completing courses of study, but in reality it was going to be difficult to launch this particular boat. This third hoop remained a problem.

The first manager to take the stage was Chris Atherly. Chris hailed from Birmingham and was a cheerful soul. If one had to say which stage character could be best likened to him, it would have to be a youthful Falstaff. Chris was indeed rather stout, with a jovial disposition which supported a great sense of humour and fun. He was also a man who lived life to the full and even, at times, a little beyond that. As these personal qualities blossomed so they characterised life early on at the hostel. Chris made it a happy hostel; but there was also a serious side to him. I judged that he was in his mid-thirties when he joined us – a youngish man but not too young. He still had plenty of youthful energy and yet did not lack for experience – a useful cocktail, and particularly so because his experience was in youth work. It soon became apparent that his experience was going to be invaluable. The cardinal

---

[3] The importance of this factor was soon realised. Young men who can hardly read do not advertise that fact. I set and marked homework for one of our residents, aged 17, while he was in prison. He was highly intelligent and almost completely uneducated. It was a joy to teach him. He made outstanding progress with his studies while in prison but flatly refused to take up a place at college after his release because of the humiliations associated with his earlier intermittent schooling and his belief that he would not be able to match the educational standards of his peers. He is presently employed as a van driver. He should be at university.
[4] We eventually overcame this problem by organising our own literacy classes.
[5] Doorstep thieving, stealing from parked cars, breaking and entering empty premises were the usual sorts of things.

virtue that Chris Atherly demonstrated from day one was that he could communicate naturally and effectively with his young men. He spoke their language (including all the four-letter words that were necessary) and he understood all their rules and shibboleths. Because of this ability to communicate, the young men soon began to confide in him and to seek his advice. They somehow grasped the fact that he was not an Establishment figure and was not likely to become one. He was as streetwise as the lads themselves, and I soon formed the impression that some of his expertise had been acquired in a similar environment to theirs. He was definitely one of us and not one of them as far as the lads were concerned. For them to find such a person in charge of a residential scenario, which must have exceeded anything that the youngsters had experienced before, ensured that the hostel would get off to a flying start – which it did. Chris Atherly was a good man to fly the first flag. Observation of his technique in dealing with our youngsters, who were variously described as 'difficult', 'undisciplined', 'lacking all moral principle', 'seriously disturbed', and 'emotionally crippled',[6] taught me much. By the time that Chris Atherly left the employ of St Matthew's Housing I knew from his example that entry into these young men's world and hearts could only be gained or earned by first establishing a relationship of trust with each of them. And having regard to my own background and history and my total ignorance of the teenage subculture which had spawned them, I knew it would require much time, much patience and no little humility on my part in seeking first to learn and only then, perhaps, to teach. Nevertheless, I knew that was the only way ahead and I was determined to give it a go.

I did not have long to wait before I had the opportunity of assessing the size of the problem that awaited me. Chris had suggested that by way of introduction I should meet the first five lads, who had just moved in, and explain to them who the Friends of Valerie Hanson House were and what their function was to be. I prepared myself well for the meeting and in my innocence was confident of success. I was not without experience in the presentation of a topic for discussion and knew that I was delivering a package which would whet the appetite of any teenager. In addition to the

---

[6] These were some of the official labels appended to those of our residents who appeared in the criminal courts.

5

financial help with further education and vocational training, which might receive a muted response, I was going to let them know what I had in mind for a programme of social and sporting events.[7] I also had a trump card up my sleeve. I had taught all four of my own teenage children to drive. Why not repeat the process with the residents? Surely, that would go down well? More importantly, a full licence to drive would be a part-way ticket to paid employment.[8]

Our meeting took place early one evening in the hotel's dining area. When I arrived the five lads were arranged down one side of the large table which dominated the dining area, leaving me to take my seat opposite them. I noted the confrontational positioning with some apprehension. It was, of course, the first time that I had met our first residents face to face. But my feelings of apprehension were quickly banished by a much stronger emotion, which took hold as I gazed into the faces of the young men that sat opposite me. If these were those whom my world had condemned and labelled as life's losers, then I was grateful to have been placed in a position where I might help them shed that unfortunate nomenclature. My hope and prayer was that with some help they would soon show my world and, more importantly, their own world that they too had qualities and skills that would enable them to make their way along the conventional paths as well as anyone. Such was the purity and innocence of my thoughts (some would say naivety) in those early days – thoughts which had prompted my own attendance at the meeting.

I noted with some amusement that Chris must have organised some sort of scrub up for my benefit. The lads were spotlessly clean even if rather poorly clad in the conventional teenage uniform of the day – slacks or jeans, sweatshirts, trainers and very little else apart from individual accoutrements by way of bracelets, necklaces, and of course, earrings. Baseball caps, a usual adornment, were conspicuously absent. Chris must have ordained it as a hats-off meeting so that I could take in the hairstyles. The hair fashion

---

[7] This would include, for example, watching Premier League football, visits to Alton Towers, go-karting, ten-pin bowling and the like – the sort of 'treats' any lad might reasonably expect from a dutiful father.

[8] Of course, almost all of our residents had been driving illegitimately for months if not years before they came to us. We had one lad, aged 16, who had been driving for four years. He had a cushion to sit on so he could see over the dashboard but, like all our other unofficial drivers, no tax, no licence and no insurance. The legitimising of our unofficial drivers was a major and never-ending task in the trek back to mainstream living.

of the day was then short-cropped though not skinhead and all but one were coiffured accordingly. Mark was the exception. He sported shoulder-length hair which was well worth sporting. Fine in texture, golden brown in colour and recently washed, it framed a fair-skinned, freckled face with clear blue eyes that definitely twinkled. I was going to like Mark. He sat in the middle of the group of five. His two close colleagues, Peter ('Pip') and Tony, sat on either side of him. Pip was a definite good-looker and knew it. His hair was thick, black, close-cropped and crinkly. He had dark-brown gypsy eyes, regular features and the high cheekbones and dark swarthy skin of a junior Romeo.[9] Tony was a very different kettle of fish. He looked much older than his years. His face was already lined and he was almost haggard in appearance. Whatever trauma he had experienced in earlier life was reflected in it. Tony also had the sort of eyes that I would soon recognise as those of a regular drug user.

Towards the end of the table sat the daddy of them all, Freddy. Topping 18 years, and the oldest of the five, he had all the airs and graces of a Mr Big. Although older than the others, he was also smaller though extremely well built. I remember thinking that he would have made an excellent loose-head prop for Northampton Saints rugger XV. I don't suppose that the thought had occurred to him or to them – a good example of some wasted talent. Sufficient to say he had all the appearance of being a hard nut. I got the uncomfortable feeling when I looked him straight in the eye that he could buy and sell me ten times over and couldn't wait for the opportunity to do just that.[10] Towards the other end of the table was Derek. He sat a little apart from the others and that's how I always viewed Derek thereafter. He was not like the others. Although he wore their garb, spoke their language and behaved in accordance with their tenets, he never seemed to belong. He was in the teenage culture but somehow not part of it. I found out why later on. He was too intelligent. In the meantime, he was the quiet man of the group.

The meeting itself was a complete disaster. The reaction of the five young men to my box of goodies, packed with care and displayed with enthusiasm, was one of almost complete indifference.

---

[9] An apt name in view of subsequent events.
[10] In the event I got off lightly. When Freddy left the hostel six months later, I lent him £20. I have never seen Freddy or the £20 since.

7

Their silence was deeply embarrassing. It was broken only by a request from Mr Big that they could smoke. There was no acknowledgement of what I had said, no questions asked as to the details and certainly no word of thanks. If they agreed with my suggestions, then they did so without the slightest sign of enthusiasm. If not, then they dismissed them without so much as a shrug of the shoulders. I might just as well have delivered my remarks in Chinese. I recall that my immediate reaction was one of resentment, even of anger. I had spent a lot of time and energy in dreaming up the concept of the Friends of Valerie Hanson House and here I was, having presented what I thought was a mouth-watering account of all the advantages that would flow for the benefit of the residents. Surely, at least a word of thanks and some degree of interest would not have been out of place? In terms of conventional good behaviour the lads had scored zero. But then I realised that at my very first encounter with them I was committing the cardinal sin of judging them by my own standards, which were not theirs. Nevertheless, I pondered for days afterwards the reason for their rebuff, before I realised that I had experienced the flip side of the coin that Chris could call so successfully. I realised that their behaviour towards me was par for the course and that I had been faced with an inevitable complete shutdown in communication. The residents were meeting me for the first time and I, unlike Chris, was obviously a fully paid-up member of the Establishment, a creature from another world to be treated with suspicion and distrust.[11] I had as yet built no relation of trust with any one of them and the door into their world was therefore tightly shut. I had no alternative but to retreat with egg on my face, resolving to do better next time.

I did not have long to wait. Within a few days, Chris suggested that we might demonstrate the effectiveness of the support that the lads might expect from the Friends. He suggested that we took them to London for a day out. He confessed that he wasn't sure as to what the reactions of the lads might be to the usual tourist attractions, but he did advance other cogent reasons why the

---

[11] It was not until I had a few years' experience under my belt that I discovered the source of this instinctive suspicion and distrust. So many of the lads came to us with the firm conviction, rightly or wrongly, that they had been badly let down by those who should have been pillars of their own Establishment – their parents, natural or otherwise, their family, their teachers, social workers and so on. As a result, they had turned to a world of their own making, where they thought they could live more comfortably – the world that we call the teenage subculture.

suggested day might be welcomed with interest and even excitement. He explained that of the five young men now in residence, none had ever been to London. Tony had never been outside Northampton and only Derek and Freddy had ever ridden on a train before. I was soon to discover that Chris was quite skilled in producing chilling statistics that strained my credulity to the limit. In those far-off days I just could not comprehend that whereas one of my own 16-year-old grandsons had just tucked away eleven A or B grades at GCSE level, in subjects ranging from Latin to Christian theology, as a prelude to almost certain entry into a major British university, there were contemporaries of his at Junction Road who were almost illiterate, had never seen London, had never ridden on a train and, in one case, had never set foot outside Northampton. Even more alarmingly, I was later to discover that some of the deprived, dispossessed, disadvantaged, dropout youngsters that passed through our hands at Junction Road were as intelligent as my own grandson. By then my incredulity had been converted into an anger directed at whatever system and whichever people were responsible for this strangulation of intellectual potential and wastage of talent.[12] But all that lay in the future. My immediate enthusiasm was for planning our expedition to London.

With just five young tourists, and Chris and I as minders, it made for what seemed to be an ideal controllable group. Surely we could open up London for discovery by our young charges? It was some years since I had 'done' London with my own children and grandchildren, but I felt I could still give a reasonable account of the history that attached to the usual tourist attractions. Such were my continuing innocence, purity of thought and downright naivety as we shepherded our young charges onto the local commuter train at Northampton Castle station bound for Euston.

The journey down to London was, of course, a first-time experience for our five young men, but it was also the first opportunity I had of observing their general demeanour and of listening to their conversation at close quarters. My learning curve would thus benefit. In those days my hearing was acute and we had managed to occupy a self-contained 7-seater section of the compartment

---

[12] Initial targets for my anger were the government educationalists of the day, and the teaching profession, whose skills relating to politics appeared to exceed those relating to teaching. A later and more mature judgement was that the fundamental causes were rooted in the collapse of responsible parenthood. This issue is dealt with in a later chapter.

which gave us some semblance of privacy and intimacy of conversation. Even so, I had great difficulty in picking up every word that was spoken. That was because all the lads spoke very quickly from mouths that hardly opened, using a modern teenage jargon that I did not fully understand and sprinkling it liberally with four-letter words some of which I had not heard since my Army days. I soon came to the conclusion that they spoke quickly because they knew they would be interrupted in midstream by a colleague who would state his case in a higher decibel so as to drown out the first speaker. Each seemed to stop talking only to draw breath and think what to say next. No one seemed to listen to anything that anyone else was saying. The cumulative effect was that everyone seemed to be talking at the same time. Nevertheless, after a few miles I was beginning to interpret and, with Chris constantly dampening down the excess in noise and the unacceptable language (which concerned Chris, embarrassed me and was totally ignored by the lads), to absorb the topics which were the subject of their conversation.

Topping the list were the subjects of pop music, cars and motorcycles, and recent exploits with their mates, the last of which appeared to cover everything from brushes with the law to alcoholic consumption on the grand scale to sexual experimentation with this one and that one. Items that never got on the list for discussion included politics and current affairs (understandable given their current blandness), sport (surprisingly) and drugs (hardly likely in the presence of an Establishment figure like me). Also off the list (which did not augur well for the day ahead) was any talk about the journey itself or the prospective wonders that awaited them in London – with one exception. The Virgin Megastore, Aladdin's cave to all pop lovers, was to be the primary (and as it turned out the only) target of their visit. Their discussions on pop music were animated and to me, the uneducated onlooker, seemed quite expert. What to me was an endless cacophony of sameness churned out by the pop industry was obviously something very different to them. The manner in which they compared, for example, one bass-guitar player with another signified perceptive ears, which surprised me. Would the perceptive ear extend to Mozart? An interesting thought. But I wisely refrained from throwing my hat into the ring and arguing the case for the Viennese classical school. Instead I listened to a passionate advocacy from Mark as to the merits of a group called Guns N' Roses, a name I have always associated with him to this day.

As with the music, so with the cars. They knew what they were talking about. And it wasn't theoretical knowledge either. Although there was an element of bravado attached to their remarks, it was apparent that every one of them had driven vehicles, even though they didn't own a single driving licence, insurance policy or tax disc between the lot of them. What they did have, each one of them, was a burning ambition to have a vehicle of their own. It seemed that in their world this represented the pinnacle of personal success and a much sought-after status symbol. What also surprised me was their apparent engineering knowledge as to what went on under the bonnet of a car. My imagination was again stirred, and I could see the same discussion taking place under the watchful eye of the tutor of mechanical engineering at Northampton College of Further Education. What sort of big stick or olive branch would we need to effect the necessary change of venue?

Of course, the lads' apparent expertise in pop music and motor engineering was heightened by my own ignorance of both subjects. Not so with Chris, who joined in vigorous discussion on both topics, another reminder that my feet were still firmly planted in my world and not theirs. As to their remarks on the subjects of alcohol and sex, I listened to a good deal of bravado and hot air promoting the macho images that were apparently so important to them. I doubted that their practice in either of these areas matched their pretensions. But I was in a new world. Anything was possible. We may well have been conveying to Euston five macho, hard-drinking, promiscuous Romeos. Certainly, that was the pattern being projected, but I doubted that it was really the case.

During our journey I also had the opportunity of studying each of the young men in turn and the interplay between them. My overall impression was that their behaviour was more a performance than reflection of who they really were, but even so it was all part of the learning process for me. There was no doubt that Freddy, the 18-year-old Mr Big, was the leader of the group. He not only led the discussions – perhaps because he shouted the loudest – but he also dominated the proceedings. He was an aggressive young man, more articulate than the others, with a confident manner among his peers nurtured by years of experience 'on the street'. He also had more than his fair share of inner anger which spilled out when he was crossed. I did not doubt his leadership of the group, only where it might lead them.[13] I certainly marked Freddy down as a difficult one to handle, but one whose personal history might explain a lot.[14]

Derek, a quieter young man more at ease with himself, was the exception to the apparent gang rule. When he crossed swords with Freddy in discussion he would not pursue his argument (which was usually well put together), but I got the clear impression that he turned away from confrontation not from respect or fear as did the others but from what appeared to be a barely concealed dislike of Freddy. An independent soul here. I thought that perhaps augured well. I put Derek down on the rationalist wing of the party. Maybe he would find his own approach to mainstream living with the minimum of help from us.[15]

It was Mark, Pip and Tony who were the true disciples of Freddy, or, as it seemed to me, of anyone else who would take their hands and lead them somewhere, or anywhere. Seemingly submissive to the will of someone like Freddy, could they not also be taken by the hand and led along a new path that could bring about the release and development of whatever natural talents and skills they might have? Why not indeed. Mark seemed to be just an open 'nice guy' character, ready to agree to anything to avoid disaffection and trouble. Pip seemed to be a deeper character, playing his cards close to his chest and thinking a good deal more than he said, but clearly intent upon avoiding confrontation with Freddy. As for Tony, he appeared to be the most troubled member of the group, saying very little as if seeking to avoid adding to the turbulence already within him and which he wore with little concealment. Such were my first-attempt pen portraits of the five young men in our charge. I hesitate to imagine what sort of pen portrait those same young men might have drawn of the old fogey that alighted with them at Euston. Fortunately, there is no record of that.

---

[13] I later realised the importance of the leadership issue in determining the overall climate of the hostel and the well-being of the residents. A leader bent on mischief would soon create a gang effect with similar bent. Of course, the opposite was also true. Other leaders could produce if not a tranquil climate, then certainly one of workable tolerance.

[14] It did. As with almost all of the lads that came into our care, Freddy's personal history and background read like a horror comic. When he came to us he had good reason to believe that 'service of self' was the only worthwhile slogan for his life. Fortunately, subsequent events caused him to modify that view.

[15] He did. Within three months he had left us and found full-time employment as a van driver with his uncle in Leicester.

At Euston my learning (and embarrassment) curve was acutely extended in dramatic fashion. If British Rail, as it was then, had held little interest or excitement for our young charges between Northampton and Euston, the London Underground system proved to be a better bet. Years previously, my nerves and patience had been sorely tried first by my children and then my grandchildren as they raced up and down the source of their new-found excitement, the London Underground escalators. I now found myself in that same position. The only difference was that those acting now like ten-year-olds were in fact young men not far off legal adulthood. I had not realised that while penned within our self-contained train compartment with Chris and myself in close attendance, the lads were very much under our physical control. At Euston, they were freed from that bondage and rushed to indulge their freedom. The escalators were a God-given plaything. As I positioned myself at the top of the main escalator (with Chris at the bottom) in an effort to restrict the disaster area, I reflected further upon the fact that these lads at 16 and 17 were doing things that my own children had been doing at half their age. It was, of course, another example of the story of their young lives so far – behind with everything, education, vocational skills, job prospects, behavioural skills, emotional security and even the use and abuse of the London Underground system. Be that as it may, it was of no concern to our fellow-travellers that morning, who were pushed, nudged, jostled and generally annoyed by the antics of what were a gang of very badly behaved teenagers. A sobering thought indeed.

When we eventually shepherded our charges onto the tube train itself, we realised that here again there was nowhere our party could keep their antics to themselves. All was in public view and hearing of their fellow travellers but the issue of accountability for one's behaviour in front of other people never arose. It was as if the fellow passengers did not exist. The crude language was not abated either in volume or content, and there was a continuous jumping up and down to exchange seats, jostling fellow passengers in the process. The boisterous behaviour was objectionable. It was soon discovered that a foot jammed in the automatic door whenever the train pulled into a station could disrupt its start/stop routine – a source of great amusement to the lads and annoyance to everyone else.

I sat directly opposite the lads while all this was going on. It was as if I had a seat in the front row of the stalls at a show that shocked me to the core. I was no longer embarrassed or humiliated. I was very very angry. Every mark of good behaviour and respect for other people which had been such an important part of my own upbringing was being flouted before my eyes by five very brash and badly behaved young men who were ostensibly in my charge. I remember thinking there and then that I had obviously bitten off more than I could chew and that the sooner I could free myself from the unhappy environment in which I had placed myself, the better. When Chris leaned over and whispered in my ear, 'We've got a bit of a job on with this lot, you know,' I thought it was the monumental understatement of the year.

And so it was that Euston and all the antics that took place there set the stage for the day ahead, which turned out to be an even greater fiasco than my first meeting with the lads. We soon discovered that our charges had as much interest in Buckingham Palace (and its occupant) or the House of Commons (and its occupants) as they had of applying for a place at Hendon Police Academy. Their one and only abiding passion was to get to the Virgin Megastore in the Strand and there invest their day's cash allowance in the purchase of the pop flavour of the month. The process of CD selection was slow and laborious, occupying some two hours. It was full of interest and excitement for the lads and extreme boredom for the two minders. There are limits to the amount of interest you can feign in a subject which bores you to death, and I reached my threshold after about half an hour, capping my performance by addressing Pip as Tony and being icily informed by Pip as to my mistake. Chris lasted a little longer, but not much. Nevertheless, the lads appeared delighted by their purchases and, after lingering at Covent Garden to watch the jugglers and buskers and snatch our fill of junk food for tea, we headed back to Euston and Northampton. It was fitting that on our return to the hostel not one word of thanks for the day out was forthcoming from any of the lads. Par for the course, I thought at the time.

I thought long and hard on the way back to Northampton and continued to do so far into that evening as to the wisdom of carrying on. I was so disheartened by events. The concept of the Friends of Valerie Hanson House was stillborn, and in personal terms so far I had scored about one out of ten with the lads. The job was obviously far bigger than I had ever realised. The day had illustrated that the problem of communication and the building of relationships was made more difficult by the lads' chronic lack of education. It wasn't the fact that they didn't know what went on in the House of Commons,[16] but rather that they didn't want to find out. It was as though they looked at life through the wrong end of a telescope or like a horse would when wearing blinkers. Their vision was thus restricted and distorted. There appeared to be no appetite or ambition or wish to discover new ideas, new interests or new fields of activity that might augment their existing interests, which appeared to be confined to pop music, motor vehicles and the passing joys of alcohol, soft drugs and sexual experimentation. But surely this was too harsh a judgement? Surely I had to persevere and dig deeper to dispel such a disappointing conclusion, which was based on such a limited experience? But how? Later that evening my thoughts became more positive, and at last I came up with a proposed course of action which at least in the short term sent me soundly to sleep that night after what had been a disaster of a day.

My thinking was that there was one activity in which I was far more expert than they were and which was of absorbing interest to each one of the lads – and to scores of other lads that were to follow after them. The activity I had in mind was driving a motor vehicle. I had driven for 40 years with a full licence free of all endorsements. They had driven off and on for maybe two years, held not one full licence between the lot of them and had accumulated enough endorsements to fill a book. If I offered driving lessons with the ultimate prize of a full driving licence, how could they refuse such an offer? My offer could also include two items from a hidden agenda. In the first place, I couldn't instruct five lads all at the same time. I would have to take them on singly. Hopefully, with no audience within hearing, the macho image and stage management of the lad in question would drop and some semblance of communication and relationship be established which could be led initially by the language of driving instructor and pupil. The second point was that a full driving licence was at least half a meal ticket for a 17-year-old youngster, because there were jobs for those who could drive. The door to orthodox living could therefore open.[17] On reflection, I think

---

[16] British general elections rarely reflect a weight of voting in excess of 60% of the electorate. Unemployed youngsters in the age bracket 18 to 23 are solid non-voters.

[17] My intention was to instruct them in the basics, taking up to a dozen lessons, and then hand over to Northampton Driving Academy, who would take them up to and (hopefully) through their theory and practical tests to gain a full licence.

that the conclusion I reached that evening, and which I put into effect the next day, was one of the best decisions I ever made during my time at Junction Road. My suggestion was welcomed with something approaching enthusiasm by the lads. I also asked for the blessing of St Matthew's Housing and this was duly given, at first reluctantly (I suppose the thought of tearaways becoming supercharged tearaways was initially off-putting), but eventually with an enthusiasm that matched that of the youngsters. As a result, over a period of almost ten years, successive young men found themselves each Sunday morning occupying the driver's seat of my old Fiat (and later an equally old Ford) for a one-hour session with me as their sole companion and instructor. Slowly but inevitably – and without rushing the fences – a relationship of trust and ready communication was built up that eventually, with much spilling of beans, enabled me to better understand the inner anger which seemed to sit at the root of so many of these young men's very being and which seemed to promote the armour plating of the macho image they wore 'on stage'. And with that understanding came a new respect for the individual and with it a powerful incentive to try and restore and rehabilitate.

Chapter Two

Adventures with Pip

'The most important thing in this life is to love and to be loved.'

Aristotle (Politics)

I cannot now remember why my first invitation to take up driving lessons was extended to Pip. Maybe it was because I viewed him as Mr Average among the group of five. If my Sunday mornings with him could bear fruit in matters of communication as well as driving instruction then maybe I would be in with a chance with the others. My guess and hope was that Pip on his own might well be a very different young man from Pip in a crowd. Certainly, as one in the group during our first meeting and the disastrous trip to London, I had found it impossible to hold any sort of meaningful conversation with him in my attempt to gain some measure of the man. As with the others, Pip would avoid eye contact and answer my conversational overtures with monosyllables. He thus projected an outward show of defensive suspicion and disinterest. It was not an attractive exterior, which was a pity because he was a handsome young man and, as later years would reveal, he could produce a grin which endeared him to all. But there was little grinning in those early days – only an introverted personality of unknown quality. No wonder that I embarked upon my first driving tuition with Pip with curiosity and interest as well as some apprehension.

I knew very little about Peter John Bailey when I took him out

17

on that first Sunday morning driving lesson. I knew only what the official record told me. During infancy, he had apparently lived a fairly normal life as the only son of his married parents, who also had an older daughter, Jenny. According to the notes, when Pip was 11 or 12 or thereabouts, his father had left the matrimonial home to cohabit with another woman. Shortly after that, Pip's mother had taken in, as her new partner, a Tunisian gentleman she had apparently met while on holiday. Immediately after this reconstruction of the family home, Pip's schooling had become spasmodic and he had been left very much to his own devices. That seemed to include going to school or not going to school as he determined. Perhaps inevitably, he had then drifted into a peer group of questionable worth who had introduced him to petty street crime. Pip and his stepfather had not got on and eventually, when he felt old enough, Pip had left home. Thereafter, he had been sleeping, at least in the short term, at the homes of his friends, including in particular that of his girlfriend. It was in these circumstances that Pip eventually found his way to Junction Road. Such were the bare facts from the official record. One pondered as to what story lay behind it. I was soon to find out.

I certainly found Pip a willing and able pupil while piloting my old Fiat around the near-deserted streets of Northampton at 9 a.m. each Sunday morning. My selection of day and time suited my own quite busy weekly programme but I could hardly expect wholehearted approval from my prospective pupils. Sunday was their long lie-in day after the indiscretions of the Saturday evening, and springing out of bed at what must have seemed the crack of dawn could not have been popular. But I have to say that of all the scores of pupils subjected to the early Sunday call over a period of nearly ten years, Pip was one of the best. I would draw up outside the hostel at 8.55 a.m. every Sunday and Pip would emerge promptly at 9 a.m., sometimes admittedly a bit bleary-eyed from his Saturday evening exertions. I remember thinking that even this in itself was a small victory. I never let him down and he responded by not letting me down. He knew that I knew that because I kept telling him so. Progress indeed. As to the driving, he was the easiest of pupils. There were really only two faults to correct – the overconfidence of youth and the bad habits picked up in the years of illegitimate driving. At first, my comments were confined strictly to the job in hand, which was the driving instruction. Pip took correction well and I was able to explain and demonstrate the points that I was making. Thus I was able to show him that I knew what I was talking about and so began to gain his respect. Gradually I was able to broaden the range of our conversation. First of all, I began to feed his ego with my confessions of ignorance as to what went on under the bonnet of the car, and I readily accepted Pip's weekly oral dissertation on the mysteries of the internal combustion engine (which in fact I found both boring and incomprehensible) as time well spent. At least it was communication of a sort, and I knew that with patience and perseverance it might grow to cover matters other than mechanical engineering. And eventually it did.

It revealed a young man deeply hurt and badly damaged by his experience during early adolescence. But, surprisingly, it also revealed a young man of considerable inner resource, who had already worked out where his salvation lay and what he had to do to bring it to fruition. Pip was no intellectual giant, but I soon discovered that he was no bloody fool either.

The official record had certainly indicated that at a pre-pubescent age Pip had been the innocent victim of his parents' marital breakdown, but it was several months into our growing relationship (which extended much beyond Pip's time at the hostel) before Pip described to me the personal tragedy of the true position. Apparently, Pip had been particularly close to his father as a youngster. Pip explained that he had hero-worshipped his father, regarded him as his role model and was, whenever possible, his constant companion and friend. Favourite of their many joint ventures was a love of freshwater fishing. The highlight of young Pip's week would be the excitement engendered by an impending weekend fishing trip with his father. It is said that fishing is a philosophy rather than a sport. Be that as it may, there is no doubt that the many hours spent by Pip with his father, friend and companion, whether fishing or philosophising, were precious and all-important to the youngster's early life and development.

Then, as with the proverbial bolt from the blue, it all came to a sudden and shattering end without notice and without explanation. Pip came home from school one day to be told by his mother that his father had left home and would not be returning. Pip had received no prior indication from his father that he was going, and he received no note or other communication from him subsequently by way of explanation.[1] It was as though the relationship between Pip and his father, so precious and important to the boy, was deemed so inconsequential to the father that he could bring it to an end without notice or explanation. That at least is how Pip construed it and that is why for years afterwards Pip carried about with him the baggage of an intense inner anger arising from the perceived rejection by his father. And, of course, the replacement of his previously revered father figure by his mother's choice of a Tunisian stepfather who seemed to engage her every attention to the exclusion of Pip was seen as an appropriate insult to add to the injury. Pip's world was at an end and he had no wish to sit among the ruins. He had therefore left what he had always considered was his home, from which he was now alienated, to face up to life without a mother or father, both of whom he considered had deserted him. His slide into an alien teenage subculture was almost inevitable.

These revelations were made to me some months after Pip had left the hostel and were the fruits of a relationship which had deepened considerably since the early days. It was ironic that in fact the relationship was much enhanced by the circumstances under which Pip left the hostel and the part that I played in that event. It had a positive effect not only upon my relationship with Pip but also with the other residents as well. The circumstances were interesting.

Late one Saturday evening, Pip, Tony and Mark were caught red-handed smoking cannabis on the hostel premises.[2] Possession and/or use of specified drugs (which included cannabis) on the hostel premises was strictly forbidden by the house rules. The St Matthew's General Committee, on becoming aware of the facts,[3] and after due deliberation, decided to reprimand all three defaulters for smoking cannabis and to expel Pip for supplying the drugs and bringing them into the hostel premises. I was not involved in the

---

[1] Not until years later, on the day that Pip was married, when he received a letter from his father, who by then was in America. Pip did not reply.

[2] They were smoking what were called spliffs, which were cigarettes made from cannabis. The drug-users' union uses a myriad of names to describe a particular drug in an attempt to stamp some sort of exclusivity on their use of it. Cannabis, for example, was also known as 'weed', 'hash' or 'grass'. The amphetamines were known as 'speed' or 'whiz' and so on.

[3] If they had not become aware, the matter might have been dealt with informally by Chris without the need to expel a lad who was in fact innocent of the charges made against him. Certainly, Chris's views on the use of cannabis were more liberal than those of the general committee. Nevertheless, an important house rule had been broken and appropriate retribution was due.

proceedings of the general committee, but I did question Pip very thoroughly about the affair on a subsequent Sunday morning jaunt.

We were by then nearing the end of Pip's driving lessons, during which our relationship had steadily evolved into something which I think both of us valued. By then I also had a little experience under my belt. I was not quite so naive as in the early days. I was therefore aware that, if I was to make a sound judgement over the affair, I would have to bear in mind three important considerations when asking Pip for his version of the affair. In the first place, I knew that, in accordance with their own codes of behaviour, each of the lads when questioned by the general committee would have told lies to their heart's content if they thought that telling lies would have got them out of trouble or protected a colleague from trouble. I had already had the unnerving experience of a lad looking at me straight in the eye and telling me a barefaced lie. I would know that it was a lie and the lad would know that I knew that it was a lie. But he would still tell me it if it furthered his ends or the ends of a colleague. That was how things were dealt with in their culture.

Next, I knew that, according to the same code, no lad would ever 'grass' (inform) on a colleague, particularly when under interrogation by any form of authority. 'Grassing' was a cardinal sin and there were no exceptions. The third factor, which was perhaps more tenuous, was my new-found relationship with Pip and the extent to which I could rely upon it. Bearing in mind these shibboleths of the subculture that Pip had embraced, and then his new-found relationship with me, which appeared to run counter to it, would I be able to extract the truth from Pip? In fact, I got halfway and was well pleased.

Pip assured me that he was telling the truth when he said that he did not bring the drugs into the hostel. He also told me that he knew who had but was unwilling to give a name. I took that to be par for the course. I told Pip that I believed him and that I trusted him. I thereupon wrote to the general committee stating that I had reason to believe that they had come to a wrong conclusion, and as a result, they were about to victimise an innocent party. I pressed the matter with some vigour[4] and subsequently wrote to the chairman of the St Matthew's Society, all of which was to no avail.

---

[4] Which included an off-the-record shouting match with the chairman in the hostel garden, witnessed by all the residents.

Significantly and depressingly, Pip saw his expulsion as yet another example of the tiresome iniquities of the Establishment world and the sort of people to whom he was expected to accord respect. I have no doubt that the weight of the inner anger he was carrying around was increased accordingly, but I was beginning to get to Pip by this time. I knew him well enough to know that, whereas he might well accept an offered spliff, he would never deal in drugs or have possession with intent to supply even for social purposes. Most important of all, he knew that I trusted him. That was real progress. It had ramifications with the other lads too. They knew who had supplied the cannabis and they knew it wasn't Pip. They also knew that I alone, outside themselves, was prepared to accept Pip's word that he was not the guilty party. They also knew that I had given him all the support that I had been able to muster. I wouldn't say that I became a hero overnight, but some of the lads were beginning to accept that I was perhaps tarred with a rather different brush from the rest of the Establishment world.

Pip's expulsion from the hostel therefore enhanced our relationship rather than impaired it. As the armour plating, now no longer necessary, began to fall to the ground to reveal the true Pip, so my respect for that young man grew. It is a wise man that knows his own limitations. Well, Pip not only knew his but had worked out just how he was going to overcome them so that he could make his way in what he considered to be an alien world. Pip was no leader among men or intellectual giant. He had little worldly ambition and no great ideals or ideologies to propel himself forward. Above all, he had no particular personal strength of will that would carry him through the difficulties that he knew lay ahead. Recognising that position with an honesty and humility that I could only admire, he had then reasoned with impeccable logic that only the acquisition of a lifelong helpmate with particular qualities could redress the balance – someone who was strong, someone who could lead, someone who could accept and discharge responsibilities and someone who could dominate him and steer him into the calm, unruffled waters of contentment for which he longed. Above all, he needed someone to love him for what he was, with all his weaknesses and shortcomings. He had tasted that fruit in early childhood and had it snatched from him as he entered early adolescence. The remedying of that loss was the greatest prize of all that a helpmate could give him. And the consideration for all these things? Only himself, his total submission, his devotion, his loyalty and his love. All this Pip had plotted and begun to set up at the age of 16 before he came to the hostel, had fashioned with enthusiasm while there and brought to full bloom thereafter. I witnessed all this as a (very prejudiced) spectator who was privileged at various times to pour oil into the workings of the grand scheme so that the wheels might spin that much faster.

Emily West, aged 15 when she first met Pip, was the only daughter and eldest child of John and Jane West, who lived only a few hundred yards from the Junction Road hostel. Emily had three brothers, and all the West children were about to reach or were already clambering up the adolescent ladder. The attendant difficulties duly proliferated. Emily's father was a skilled engineer who had been faced with early redundancy. His wife Jane worked part-time, a necessary arrangement to help in the everlasting battle to make the financial ends meet. Shortly before Emily met Pip, one of her brothers, Robert, had been knocked down in a road accident and suffered irreversible brain damage. It seemed that the married life of John and Jane West was one of frantic endeavour and constant crisis. It says much for their calibre that in spite of all their difficulties their marriage remained solid, their home inviolable and the respect of their children constant. Thus are the proud humbled by such an example. And Emily West was a chip off the old block. A big, busty, good-looking young woman,[5] she was strong, she was organised, she was energetic and she was very determined. She was just about everything that Pip was not. She lacked only one thing to complement these many virtues – a soulmate to mother, to smother, to dominate and to lead by the hand upwards to the sunlit plateau which she assuredly believed was awaiting her and her partner.

Pip met Emily at a weekend party. Pip sensed that Emily might be the answer to all his prayers. Emily knew that Pip was the answer to all of hers. Pip was 16, Emily 15. Within a week they were inseparable – and they have remained so ever since. Of course, there is no doubt that sexual activity was a major factor in their relationship. Insofar as it comprised the physical expression of the need and love for each other, it was inevitable. Pip was a handsome, healthy and virile young man, and I knew from sources other than

---

[5] 'Plenty to catch hold of' was an early disrespectful remark by Pip.

him that he was sexually experienced. Sex was never a problem to him and there were no moral or psychological overtones that blunted the enjoyment of its practice as far as he was concerned. I remember him once saying to me that the great thing about sex was that it was free. Other pleasures – a night at the cinema or the pub – were enjoyable, but they cost. Sex did not. He was aware of the dangers of sexual disease but would have nothing to do with condoms, which he once described as 'masking the true beauty of the act'. He always said that he had picked his sexual partners with care and ensured that they were 'on the pill'. It is noteworthy that after he met Emily there was no further picking of partners. He had found his partner for life. As to Emily's reaction to Pip's physical approaches, I cannot say, except that I was aware of some of the more hilarious instances under which these physical unions occurred.

It was, for example, a regular practice of Pip's in his pre-hostel days to shin up the drainpipe which ran alongside Emily's bedroom at the rear of the West residence and spend the night cosying up to Emily. Of course, the lovebirds had to have their wits about them first thing in the morning when Emily's mother would come along the landing to give her daughter her early morning call. At the critical moment, Pip would slide gently from the duvet that engulfed them both and deposit himself under the bed.[6] Also remembered are occasions when Pip would set out from the hostel to do his day's work, clad in his overalls with snack tin to hand, only to move a few hundred yards onto Northampton Racecourse, where he would meet up with Emily. She would be carrying a tent, which they would then pitch to give them the required privacy. Pip would then reappear at the hostel at 5 p.m. at the end of his day's work complaining how exhausted he was. He may well have been. On another famous occasion, I called at the hostel to pick up the lads who made up our five-a-side soccer team for their usual Tuesday training session. Alas, the five-a-side team consisted of four individuals. The missing star was Pip, but I needed only one guess to know where he would be. Knocking on the door of the West residence a few minutes later, I was confronted after a while by my tousle-headed, bleary-eyed midfield player. When reminded that

---

[6] Of course, the inevitable was bound to happen and did. There is no record of Jane's expression when she failed to make enough noise as she came along the landing one morning and discovered the two lovebirds soundly asleep in each other's arms.

he was required for football practice, he advised me that he couldn't possibly make it that evening because, Jane and John being out for the evening with the other children, he was in bed with Emily. Football was obviously not his abiding interest at that moment. I departed with a flea in my ear, musing as to the sexual splendour of youth.

If Pip's sex life therefore blossomed in a relationship where the physical union became more and more a reflection of a union beyond that, there also existed, nevertheless, other different issues which Pip had to face to which Emily could give only her moral support. In particular, and as a first priority, Pip had to get a job and earn real money if he was ever going to live independently with Emily. It was, of course, the same problem that confronted all the young men who came to us so short of basic education and vocational skills. It was also a problem which demanded and received much of my own time and efforts over the years. However, in the case of Pip, he did give me a lead. He told me that during the school holidays he had often taken up casual work on local farms and had enjoyed the harvesting activities. He had also made it clear on more than one occasion that the outdoor life was the one for him. Armed with this information, my emotions played a few tricks on me. I had visions of our future farmworker returning home from the day's harvesting in his Land Rover to be welcomed and embraced by Emily and their four children at the door of their rose-scented thatched cottage nestling in the English Cotswolds with the evening meal bubbling on the hob. But how to turn this fanciful dream into a reality? Well, we could make a start. With Pip's agreement, I was soon calling upon, first of all, the local but nationally renowned Moulton Agricultural College and then upon Hugh Lowther.

Hugh was the son of the Lord Lieutenant of Northamptonshire, who had formally opened the hostel and given his blessing to our intended work with young people. Hugh farmed some thousand acres of rich farmland near the village of Guilsborough, a local beauty spot a few miles north of Northampton. I reasoned that if the college could teach and Pip could learn the rudiments of good husbandry, and Hugh Lowther could embroider the rudiments with the practicalities of modern farming, then Pip might be in with a chance to convert the dream into a reality. I also made the welcome discovery that Pip's introduction into the world of farming could be undertaken and partly financed under the umbrella of a government scheme for youth employment which was then in vogue to encourage just the sort of enterprise that we had in mind. Pip was willing, as was Hugh on the understanding that Pip stuck with his college course at Moulton.

There was a slight hiccup at the college when I went there to explain Pip's circumstances and register him as a student. Apparently, Pip had previously been a student at the college – a fact that he had conveniently forgotten to mention to me. On that occasion he had been expelled, aged 15, having been found 'in a state of undress' with a female student in one of the college's own barns. I expressed appropriate horror and surprise, which was hardly warranted in view of my foreknowledge of Pip's sexual athleticism. Nevertheless, after plugging hard the fact (?) of Pip's new-found maturity, it was agreed that a new Pip file would be opened and the old one shredded. He was then duly registered as a student.

That overcame one problem, but two further problems remained. Although Pip had passed his driving test by this time and had a clean driving licence, he had no vehicle or the means to acquire one, let alone tax and insure it and supply it with fuel. How then would he report for duty at Hugh's farm each morning? The other snag was that Pip's weekly cash entitlement under the government scheme was limited to £40 for the four days' work on the farm and one day at college. Pip had long since left the hostel by the time these arrangements were coming to fruition and was leading an almost gypsy-like existence, moving from one kind of accommodation to another as the occasion and his pocket demanded. It was obvious that, if his weekly income was to be restricted to £40, nothing would remain in his pocket after payment of all dues and demands. Financially, the venture was therefore impossible. In fact, both problems were solved following a further interview with Hugh, with Pip in attendance.

Hugh made it clear that following the training period, and assuming that Pip shaped up, a permanent job would become available at the full rate of pay. Both Pip and I could therefore see that a real opportunity of permanent employment in a field that engaged Pip's declared interest and enthusiasm was possible. Somehow, the problems which were related to the training period alone had to be resolved. And they were. I agreed to ferry Pip to Guilsborough and back to Northampton each day, and Pip agreed to make his peace with his mother and her new partner and take up residence with them. He

26

would hope then for some sort of subsidised arrangement as regards board and lodging. This would at least ensure that there would be something left in his pocket each week out of the £40. Pip's mother was pleased to welcome him back on a subsidised basis, and so a daily routine of collection and delivery from and to her residence was commenced.

Each morning at 8 a.m. I would be parked outside the reconstituted family home and within minutes Pip would appear, overall-clad and snack tin in hand. Half an hour later he was at the farm reporting for work. He was never late. Collecting times at Guilsborough varied according to how the work had gone. A telephone call from Pip was the signal. At harvest time the call did not come until the light was fading. Pip was invariably exhausted when I picked him up and sometimes not all that popular. Those were the occasions when he had been on his fortnightly tractor run to a neighbouring farm to collect loads of chicken manure for transfer to Hugh's farm. Samples of the merchandise were inevitably deposited on Pip's boots and thereby inevitably deposited on my car upholstery. This sort of self-induced mishap was a comparatively minor matter, but in retrospect one ponders at the wisdom or otherwise of taking matters to the extreme lengths that we did to launch Pip at Guilsborough. At the time, the prize was great – a permanent job and every prospect of advancement. But there was more to it than that, and of even greater importance, although no one realised it at the time.

Guilsborough saw the seeds of self-knowledge grow as far as Pip was concerned, which changed his whole attitude towards honest toil, its need, its worth and, indeed, its dignity. After Guilsborough, Pip could always look hard work in the face and get up in the morning and get on with it in the knowledge that he could do it as well as the next person. At Guilsborough itself within a few weeks he was being hailed as a 'natural'. He took to all the practical work like the proverbial duck to water. Within months he was driving tractors like an old hand and could handle most of the other farm machinery as well. He could cut hedges, plough, cultivate and harvest. He could even drill a field with seed corn under supervision. He could also put his hand to all the countless jobs of farm maintenance like fencing and building and machinery repairs, and he got on well with his fellow workers while he did so. Even more surprisingly, he was applying himself diligently to his course

27

of study and practical work at Moulton.[7] I could see the prospects of a full-time job for life growing by the day as Pip got more and more experience under his belt.

I vividly recall one particular occasion during this period of high hopes. It made me think that all the effort had been worth it, that Pip had been well and truly launched and that I might begin to turn my thoughts and efforts away from him towards other young men at the hostel and their problems. The particular image that I have in mind – and it is one that will always remain there as a memory of Pip – is of a late summer evening at harvest time. I had received my usual telephone call from Pip to collect him, and half an hour later I sat in my car on the road which bisected Hugh's farm. It was a beautiful evening in mid-September. The countryside was still in full bloom albeit with the autumnal colours just beginning to encroach. A benign warmth lingered from a day now fading that had kept the band of harvesters hard at it and lathered in sweat from dawn to dusk. The only sound was the throaty roar of a combine harvester coming from a field of half-cut corn to my left. I could not see the combine because the field dipped away quite steeply as it left the road where I was parked. The first sighting I had as the combine roared up the hill was therefore not of the monster itself but of a tiny figure perched on its top, encrusted with dirt, dust and straw but clearly silhouetted against the setting sun. As the combine roared into sight, so the small figure identified himself by waving and shouting above the roar of the engine, 'Are you all right, Smithy?' At that moment I could have reassured Pip that I was not just all right but would be better described as 'over the moon', so pleased, so glad and so proud I felt then for Pip. I felt that we had come a long way since the early days. I contented myself by shouting back to Pip, 'Yes, I'm all right, are you?' It was a silly question because I knew the answer only too well. Pip roared away down the hill.

Alas, the Guilsborough tale did not have a fairy-tale ending. One evening, when visiting my flat with Emily for dinner, Pip told me that he had been offered and had accepted a job in a local engineering works which would earn him over £160 per week. He said that he had been approached on more than one occasion over the last three

---

[7] I once watched him shearing a sheep. An Australian sheep farmer would have been pleased to take him on.

months or so by a neighbour who was employed at the works and he had finally agreed to make the application, which had been accepted. While I was devastated by what I thought and said was a bad decision, I understood only too well why these two young people, now aged 18 and 19, had made the decision that they had. They were, after all and quite simply, very much in love and they wanted to live together. They could do that on £160 weekly. They could not do it on £40 weekly. As with modern youngsters the world over, they were not prepared to wait.

There was also another factor. Life with Pip's mother and partner had apparently deteriorated into a daily slanging match, and the sleeping arrangements were primitive to say the least. The two bedrooms were taken up by his mother and her partner and by Pip's sister. Pip had been sleeping downstairs on a camp bed. I argued long and hard in favour of Guilsborough and the near certainty of a job at the end of his training, which on Pip's own admission would have been the ideal solution, but I knew I was on a loser. It was the immediate position which was the most important to the youngsters. I dragged Pip over to Guilsborough to see if Hugh could prevail upon him any better than I had done. He did not. So Pip left the outdoor job on the farm at Guilsborough that he loved so much and disappeared into the bowels of a large engineering works. Nevertheless, when he emerged at the end of the week he was clutching his £160 and there was no answer to that.[8]

It was not until I had finally come to terms with my own bitter disappointment at events that I realised that in fact a great victory had been won. The daily routine which had been part of the Guilsborough story – the getting out of bed in the morning, the getting to work, the daily toil and, above all, the realisation by Pip that he could learn to do a job and do it well – was such a revelation to the young man himself that he recovered much of the self-esteem and confidence he had lost in early adolescence. Pip had learnt that he could do a job, earn money and take his place in the real world. He no longer had need of the twilight world of a previous subculture. Of course, the decision to give up Guilsborough was a wrong one, but in the bigger scheme of things Pip had arrived. That was more

---

[8] Other than a more enlightened attitude from a government that had spawned the Youth Training Scheme in the first place without funding it properly.

important than anything. After all, that was the purpose of the exercise in the first place.

And so Pip and Emily lived happily ever after – or at least they have done so up to the time of going to press. They acquired a council house, an old banger car and the most beautiful little daughter that God ever made, called Claire. And last but not least, they were married.[9] The wedding was at Kingsthorpe Church (where my own parents were married) with all the trimmings, and I viewed the proceedings with true thanksgiving, happiness and pride. As to life thereafter, I believe that Emily manages the shop and Pip as well. That is an arrangement convenient to them both. Pip changes his job frequently with the sure touch of the gypsy that he always was and suffers occasional twinges of Guilsborough nostalgia. But he works and earns. I suspect that each week his earnings are tipped out on the kitchen table and Pip is then allocated his weekly pocket money before the rest disappears into the chancellor's treasure chest. If so, they are not the only couple that arrange their finances so, and in any case that is none of my business. Pip wanted so little out of life – just to love and be loved. He found that happy arrangement with his Emily. Long may it last.

---

[9] So, in conventional terms, they got the order a bit mixed up. Never mind, the sacramental union when it came was truly one in flesh and spirit until 'death do them part'.

Chapter Three

Life and Times at Junction Road

'Experience is the essential child of Thought and Thought is the child of Action. We cannot learn about men from books.'
Benjamin Disraeli (1826)

My adventures with Pip extended over a period of years and far beyond his time at the hostel. The lessons learned were invaluable. Many of the problems of those young men who followed on after Pip were but variations of the Pip theme – much inner anger and resentment born of past hurt usually masked by macho behaviour and manifested in an opting-out from mainstream living.

There had been no quick fix to Pip's problems. They were deep-seated, very personal and rooted in that young man's past. There had been no quick fix either to the dismantling of Pip's external armour plating and its replacement by a personal trust and faith in those who were prepared to help him.[1] And so it was with those that followed. Much patience and perseverance would be necessary to break through the outer protective crust, which unfortunately included so many disagreeable and unattractive features. Many of the young men that came to us displayed an aggressive, albeit feigned, attitude of self-sufficiency often manifested in an unwelcome cockiness and an accountability for their actions owed to no one

---

[1] Politicians, please note. Rehabilitation of young men who have forsaken mainstream living for the teenage subculture has nothing to do with political soundbites, or 20-minute magisterial homilies, or custodial sentences. It has everything to do with long-term and painstaking care and understanding leading ultimately to the essential trust that will form the basis of rehabilitation.

but themselves. They seemed to have precious little respect but rather a profound suspicion and distrust of everyone but their own peers. There was very seldom any contribution to social awareness, or conscience, and it was therefore not surprising that some of these young men considered that compliance with the law of the land was a matter of personal choice. And these unwelcome and unsocial characteristics were usually accompanied by the equally disagreeable trappings of ill manners and foul language. Of course, there were conspicuous exceptions, but they only served to prove what was an unfortunate general rule.[2] It was not an attractive package, and it was therefore perhaps understandable that those caught up in the serious business of mainstream living should have little time, and less inclination, to adopt any attitude toward those they considered to be social outcasts other than keeping them at a distance and preferably out of sight.[3] They were not to know that under a brash and unattractive exterior there was often a deeply hurt and frightened young man in desperate need of help to repair his damaged self-esteem and develop his inherent talents.

I knew that with that help these young men were quite capable of becoming fully paid-up members of the mainstream community. The sight of Pip Bailey perched on top of a combine harvester at Guilsborough had taught me that, and if it could be done for Pip then it could be done for others. Now that he had shown me the way ahead, a good deal of the dejection and disappointment of the early days could be buried. I was more than ever determined to learn from my experience as I went along, and to ride my luck.

As with Pip, my main weapon in breaking down the defensive outer crust which so many of our young men seemed to sport was the offer of driving lessons. Sure enough, as soon as I announced this appetiser, an immediate queue began to form.

The driving lessons themselves were comparatively uneventful and, in terms of end result, eminently successful. Although we were insured up to the eyeballs, we hit nothing during nearly ten years of tuition. That was because my pupils wanted to learn, were the

---

[2] Unsurprisingly, we had more than our fair share of bedwetters among those who were the most aggressive, a clear indication of outward shell and inner self.

[3] The Young Offenders detention unit at Glen Parva, near Leicester (reputed at one time to be the dirtiest prison in the United Kingdom) and at Onley, near Rugby, served this purpose well. Over the years, there was always one or more of our residents, past or present, incarcerated in one of these institutions from the age of 16 upwards.

right age to learn and were genuinely interested in the whys and wherefores of effective driving. My job was therefore made easy. My old Fiat was not fitted with dual controls so we kept off the highways, even though the traffic was scarce on a Sunday morning.[4] We would perform manoeuvres on various parking lots and were regularly moved from one empty space to another as successive security guards, resplendent in their peak caps and brandishing their authority, announced our act of trespass.[5] Over the years I must have taught the basic driving techniques to between 40 and 50 lads before handing them over to the academy to add the finishing touches and groom them for the formal driving test. When that great day arrived I always contrived to have a word with the lad concerned to give him such tactical advice as to convince the examiner that he was not examining the local tearaway. I usually advised the need for a close control on language as well as speed and that it would be wise on the day to leave their baseball caps behind, divest themselves of their earrings and address the examiner as 'Sir'. It was perhaps indicative of our relationships by then that I could make such outrageous suggestions and gain their ready acceptance. Certainly, with or without the assistance of these tactical matters, our success rate was high; I can only remember two or three young men who never graduated. A young man called Pete, aged 18, cut short his lessons and fled north with the police in hot pursuit. Michael[6] had to abandon his lessons on taking up residence at Onley Young Offenders Unit, and Eric just faded away.

Eric was a young man, aged 18, with homosexual tendencies. He constantly asked permission for Bob, his friend and partner, to accompany him on his lessons, which I explained was against the rules. Eric wore very large 'bovver' boots, which were not at all helpful in operating the pedals. After I had explained that sensitive feet were the mark of a good driver, I asked him to change them, but he explained that they were the only footwear he had, and in

---

[4] Their 'in traffic' tuition was undertaken by the driving academy after completion of the basic course with me. The academy fees were paid by the Friends and there was therefore no cost to the lads.

[5] These recurrent interruptions to our Sunday morning activities were never anything other than absurd. On acres of space, our lone vehicle, insured against every eventuality, was engaged in a peaceful, innocent and recreational exercise of considerable value to the community in the long run. Who was it that said, 'All property is theft'?

[6] Michael Daly, our lovable rogue (see Chapter Six). We recommenced after the interruption and today he is the proud owner of a window-cleaning round and a clean driving licence.

any case, he needed them as some protection against threatened muggings from his homophobic brethren. Such is the world in which we live. After lessons way beyond the normal number, Eric was handed over to the driving academy, who had as little success with him as I had. He never did finish his course. He did, however, find full-time employment doing computer work and duly departed to live independently and, I hope, happily ever after with his partner Bob.

Towards the end of my time at the hostel, a theory test was introduced as part of the requirements for a full driving test certificate. This created a difficulty with our lads. Theory, which involved academic learning, was not and never would be second nature to them, and the theory test produced more chewed-up fingernails and discarded cigarette butts than the practical test ever did. The memory of one lad stands out in particular. Aged 23, recently released from prison, where he had served time for attempted murder, and with a reputation on the street as a 'hard man', he sat in my car, sucking his thumb and seeking constant reassurance from me as we approached the test centre. His particular difficulty, the cause of his near panic, was that that at the ripe old age of 23 he had never sat an examination of any kind in his life either at school (a part-time occupation for him) or anywhere else. He was (understandably) panic-stricken at the thought that he was about to face his first. Again, I was struck by the contrast between the outer shell and the inner self.[7]

There was a pleasing postscript to the adventures with the driving lessons. One of my very early pupils was a 17-year-old lad called Kevin. Kevin was very long and very lanky and when he arranged his driving seat for a comfortable position he would adjust it to almost full recline. The effect was such that he looked as though he was driving the vehicle while still in bed. He also had difficulty in steering. He was inevitably late in the straightening up after cornering, then overcorrected and finished up with a tendency to snake the car. I remember thinking that if there was a difficulty with steering, we weren't in with much of a chance with the finer points. So there was a big sigh of relief when Kevin eventually emerged with a full licence. Nearly ten years after the event, a long-distance heavy-goods vehicle as big as the block of flats in

---

[7] There was a happy outcome. The theory test was successfully negotiated and self-esteem pushed along in the right direction.

which I live pulled up outside my front door, and out of the cab jumped this giant of a man who crushed my hand with his handshake and announced that it was the return of the prodigal, Kevin Timpson. He explained that he had been driving HGVs for a matter of four or five years and was currently earning in excess of £400 weekly. That day he had deliveries to make in Northampton and he had called especially to see me and thank me for those early driving lessons, which had led on to such a successful career. I asked him if he still had difficulty with his steering. He suggested that I follow him into town, find the busiest roundabout and then see for myself. I declined his offer. But it was moments like that when everything that we were doing, or trying to do, seemed to make sense.

During all that time spent each Sunday morning on the near-deserted parking lots of Northampton I worked assiduously, but I hope with patience and understanding, at building up some sort of relationship with each of my pupils. It was, of course, easier with some than with others. Some were forthcoming, others less so. They also came from very different backgrounds. In terms of ethnicity, our young men came in all colours, white, black, brown, and in one case yellow. In religion, we had dogmatic atheists, compliant Catholics, barnstorming Jehovah's Witnesses and any number of 'don't knows' and 'don't cares'. There was, however, among all this diversity one common factor that linked them all together. They were all the products of broken homes and they all carried with them the baggage that went with that unfortunate status.[8] An indication as to what that baggage comprised was brought home to me one Sunday morning with shocking effect and left behind an aftertaste of acute personal embarrassment. My pupil was a young Geordie called Michael, aged 17. I had taken him out for several weeks, but he was unduly reticent (although an above-average driver). I had signally failed to loosen his tongue on any subject other than the driving,[9] he was failing to laugh at

---

[8] I can call to mind only one lad where that was not the case. David, aged 16, was the eldest of four small children whose mother had died. The Department of Social Services had decided in their wisdom that the father could not cope and that the children of this close-knit and well-integrated family should be taken into care. David came to us. He was a model resident. He obtained work as an engineering apprentice, studied for his examinations, obtained his driving licence and acquired a sensible and devoted girlfriend. A role model, indeed, but rooted in a very different background to our other young men.

[9] I found with most young men that an opinion as to the respective merits of Arsenal and Manchester United was sufficient to get things started.

my rather weak jokes and he would give no opinion as to life at the hostel. Eventually, and foolishly, I said, 'Michael, you hold your cards very close to your chest. Is there nothing that I can say that will make you laugh or cry?' His reply was devastating. 'Smithy,' he said, 'if I started to cry, I would never stop.' My apologies were immediate and totally inadequate, my remorse overwhelming. I found out later that Michael had been sexually abused by both his stepfather and his stepbrother after his natural father had left him and his mother. This was the cancer that constituted Michael's baggage. I was to find that similar outrages were not uncommon in the personal histories of my other pupils.

It soon became apparent that the clean driving licence that could be earned from the driving sessions was the best bet for obtaining paid employment.[10] The source from which we expected much – the taking up of courses of study and/or vocational training – proved disappointing. The reason has already been explained in an earlier chapter. Our young men were in general poorly educated in basic literacy and numeracy. Some were even totally illiterate. Quite understandably, they were unwilling to suffer the humiliation of displaying their shortcomings while sitting in a classroom with their peers. Again, the reason for their educational weaknesses lay in their past. In most cases, because of their domestic circumstances, their school attendance had been spasmodic at best. No particular standards of basic education were reached and no certificates of any worth were held. The tragedy was that as my relationship with these young men grew, I began to realise just how intelligent some of them were. Some time ago, a well-known Member of Parliament[11] made the interesting comment that many of the members on the opposite (Tory) benches appeared to be 'educated beyond their intelligence'. At Junction Road we had the far more distressing and opposite cases of intelligent young men devoid of basic education. In later years, we attempted to remedy the problem of illiteracy 'in house', and I spent many hours giving private tuition to youngsters who could not read, write, spell or enumerate. None of them would

---

[10] To this day (April 2004), I still see 'old boys' driving their way around Northampton and district and on the motorways in everything from HGVs to Parcelforce or *Chronicle & Echo* vans, including in one case a Securicor van piloted by an ex-resident who had spent some time at Her Majesty's pleasure in Onley Young Offenders Unit. How reformed can a character get?

[11] Mr Dennis Skinner, Labour MP for Bolsover.

attend classes and all implored me to teach them privately. Only they knew the embarrassment and humiliation that they faced when confronted with the completion of simple job-application forms, or a routine enquiry from Social Security, or the need to write a simple letter. And such was the bar to further education. Time after time arrangements were made in the early days for residents to attend courses at the local college of further education, and time after time we encountered active opposition, complete disinterest or fading enthusiasm as soon as they found themselves in a class with others. Of course, opposition to formal education was one of the shibboleths of the teenage subculture in any case, and it did not help matters that most of our residents came to us with that view firmly in place.

However, we did have exceptions and these were greeted with undisguised joy. Allan, aged 17, was employed by a firm of air-conditioning and ventilating engineers, and he took to computer-assisted design work in that industry like a duck to water, his feet firmly planted on the first rung of the promotion ladder. But perhaps the best example of the exception to the rule was a young man called Matthew, aged 16, who came to us following the breakup of his family home. Matthew's trauma was manifested in a most unusual manner. He would eat to excess and become very obese. Then he would do the opposite, eating almost nothing until he was seriously underweight. This yo-yo existence was very distressing for all concerned and particularly for Matthew, who was mercilessly ribbed by his peers. He was, however, a ready pupil with the driving lessons, and he made good progress. During the course of an early-Sunday-morning conversation I asked him about his school career. In reply, he told me that he had always attended school regularly and had notched up several passes at the higher grades in his GCSE examinations. Although he struck me as a much quieter and more polished individual than was usually the case, I treated his reply with some scepticism, having by then some experience of the flights of fancy that often masqueraded as statements of fact from the young gentlemen with whom I was dealing. I asked Matthew to bring the documentary evidence showing his GCSE results the next Sunday. He did. They showed precisely what he had described the previous week. At the same time, Matthew had secured work as a clerk with a local firm of property developers. After very little pressure, Matthew was persuaded to take up a full-time course of

37

study at the Northampton College of Further Education, reading English, Sociology and Psychology at A level. After a year (during which the eating disorder made its final exit) I attended the college with Matthew[12] and met his two tutors. I was thrilled to receive their report. I was told that Matthew's work for his first year of A-level studies was up to an A-grade standard, and if he maintained that level throughout his second year he would be worthy of entry into a major university. I could hardly believe my ears. Were we about to witness the transfer of our Matthew from the frenzied activity at Junction Road to the cloistered calm of Oxford? It was moments like this one which acted as superchargers to all our continuing efforts. Alas, with Matthew it was not to be. Enter the *femme fatale*.

Kit was herself the product of a broken home and well known to our residents.[13] She was physically attractive, buxom and fair-skinned. She was also a generous, warm-hearted girl. No doubt she brought to Matthew as he brought to her the love, warmth and protection that they were both seeking. At first, the liaison was encouraged, but more fed on much until nothing else seemed to matter. Eventually, and in spite of the strongest advice to the contrary, the A levels went out of the window and Matthew left the hostel to live independently with Kit.[14] As my dear old mother used to say, 'Life is full of disappointments.' And so it is, and Matthew's performance proved it.

Of course, Matthew was an exception in having outstanding academic ability, but we certainly did have candidates who would have made the grade at a good grammar school or its modern equivalent if they had come from the same sort of stable family that I had and if they had received the full benefit from early education. The nation's loss in undeveloped skills from this source is grievous; the loss to the individual lad in terms of self-confidence and esteem almost irretrievable. If a simple lesson is to be learned,

---

[12] The occasion was Parents' Day. Matthew asked me to attend and I did so. Some amusement, or was it embarrassment, was caused when Matthew introduced me as his '70-year-old friend' to his two tutors. They perhaps thought, 'Have we some sort of improper relationship on our hands here?' Fortunately, we were all able to enjoy the joke after Matthew had explained the position.

[13] Intimately so in one case. She had borne a child by one resident when they were both 16.

[14] It proved to be very much an on/off and up/down relationship. After the inevitable child arrived there were money troubles, but eventually Matthew settled down in full-time employment as an accountant and Kit found part-time employment with the social services.

it is that responsibility for the education of children should not lie with politicians or educationalists but with the child's parents.

Having used the driving lessons to establish some sort of individual relationship with each of my young pupils, I found I was able to converse with them as a group to far better advantage than in the early days. I began to be accepted as part of the group and there was more of the 'we' and less of the 'you' and 'us' about their behaviour. With this welcome change of attitude apparent, we launched into our original programme of social and sporting activities, all of which were to be funded by those generous donors who made up the Friends of Valerie Hanson House. Our aim was twofold. We wished to provide our young men with the sorts of treats and outings that they might reasonably expect from dutiful but not overindulgent parents. We also wished to arrange informal evening talks on subjects relating to the residents' health and welfare. We had in mind alcohol, drugs and sexual health as priorities. On the first count, however, we straightaway marked the calendar with each lad's birthday and made sure that the day would not pass without due celebration, the traditional birthday cake and, of course, an appropriate birthday present. Our aim was to make the birthday boy feel important and the day a very special one for all of us for that reason. I hope we succeeded. The birthday present was invariably an item of clothing, which always figured prominently in each lad's priorities. His weekly cash budget did not extend beyond a packet of cigarettes (or roll-ups), a couple of pints of beer and his personal toiletries. There was nothing left for clothing.[15]

I think that the best birthday treat that we ever organised was the one that marked Derek's 18th birthday. As well as attaining his majority, Derek was the first of our residents to pass his driving test. There was thus cause for something special by way or celebration. It so happened that I had an ex-client who was the grandfather of a professional racing driver, himself little more than a teenager. Although not in the Formula One class, he certainly raced at Silverstone and, unknown to Derek, we were able to arrange for him to spend a day in the pits on a Silverstone race day. To Derek, it was like spending a day in heaven. There was icing on the cake too. After the racing, my client's grandson drove Derek back to

---

[15] After payment of his board and lodging (which was subsidised by housing benefit), each lad was left with about £13–15 weekly from his social security benefits.

the hostel. Perhaps he whetted Derek's appetite to follow in his footsteps. Certainly, it was a day that I am sure Derek will always remember.

Our social and sporting activities were many and various but always strictly conditional upon good behaviour both at the hostel and at the event itself. As our plans became more and more ambitious, this requirement had an increasingly beneficial effect in that the one or two loose cannons that usually figured in our number were subjected to the pressure to behave by the others so as not to prejudice the programme of 'treats'. Our outings soon included attendance at Premier League football matches (Manchester United, Liverpool and Arsenal vying for the lads' affections), go-karting, ice and roller skating (often not an elegant sight), swimming, cricket coaching, indoor bowling, visits to the cinema (and in one case to a theatre) and, of course, the theme park at Alton Towers.[16] Again, it was interesting to watch the interplay of each young man with the peer group and how some would lead and others would follow. It was not always the 'hard man' who led the way onto the most frightening of the Alton Towers contraptions. But it was good to see them let off steam in a fairly controlled manner, and they certainly enjoyed what was for most of them a totally new experience of such places of amusement and recreation.

It was during the swimming sessions that we used to arrange each fortnight that I learned yet again how easy it was innocently to say the wrong thing, and also just how these young men carried with them the scars from their past (in this case, literally). A new lad, Tim, had joined us for our swimming session but declined my invitation to swim. The same thing happened on the next visit, but after that I no longer pressed the matter. I realised that I had probably said too much already. I certainly had. I later found out that the lad didn't wish us to see the heavy bruising and scarring across his back and shoulders where he had been beaten. He was a very introverted lad and when he first came to us he could hardly put two words together. He was also a persistent bedwetter. Fortunately, he benefited much from his stay with us, which was due in no small measure to the dedicated mothering he received from Rose

---

[16] We found that obtaining tickets for some of these events, normally very difficult, was made easier by the ready cooperation we received when the particular circumstance of our applications was explained – that the tickets were required for youngsters at a hostel for the homeless. Needless to say, we did not pull our punches with these applications.

Stewart, house manager at the time. Thanks to her, he was a very different young man when he left us a year later.

As to the swimming itself, most of the lads had little idea about swimming skills, and, although I tried hard to get those who had some idea to instruct those who had none, I was fighting a losing battle. 'Never mind the swimming, get on with the fun' seemed to be the maxim. The chief attraction at the Wellingborough baths was the springboard, and there was a constant queue to see who could be the first to propel themselves through the roof of the baths. Some dived off the board, others jumped, and the others who could do neither just fell into the water. I was constantly involved in mental arithmetic to confirm that the complete party was afloat or thereabouts. It was all very nerve-racking and there was little, if any, serious swimming. It was hardly Olympic stuff. There was, however, one exception to our general standard of mediocrity and it came from a most unexpected quarter.

We had at that time a long, lanky lad in residence called William. I think William would have ranked among the leaders as one of the laziest young men we ever had at Junction Road. It was not that he got in any trouble at the hostel; it was just that he drew the line at anything that looked like, or smelled like, honest toil. He made us all despair. When eventually I inveigled him to join our fortnightly swimming sessions I must have thought it likely that, being too lazy to swim, having entered the water he would assuredly sink quietly and gently to the bottom of the pool and expire. I could not have been more wrong. Appearing last from the men's changing rooms in the briefest of bathing briefs, William entered the water with a graceful racing dive and proceeded to swim three lengths of the bath with a powerful, effortless (of course) and, as far as I could see, perfect crawl stroke. The simple fact was that long, lanky, lazy William could swim with all the grace, speed and power of a professional. I could not believe my eyes any more that the rest of his peer group, who had halted their usual antics to stare in astonishment. Here was William, the man we believed had little or no talent at anything, demonstrating the lie that left us all gob-smacked. When asked to explain his performance, he explained that swimming had been the only thing that interested him at school but he had 'never taken it up seriously since then'. The mind boggled at the thought of where he would be if he had.

The very next day, I had William performing at Northampton

41

Mounts Baths in front of the senior instructor of Northampton Swimming Club. He fully confirmed my first impressions. In his view, William was a 'natural', with a potential that could lead to the highest professional standard providing – and here was the caveat – William was prepared to undergo a programme of assiduous training and obtain peak physical fitness. And I knew, of course, that here was the snag. The world is full of people whose ambitions outstrip their abilities and much trouble is caused thereby but William was the opposite case. He had fantastic ability and yet was brain-dead as far as ambition was concerned. If I gave him one pep talk as to the opportunities now being presented to him and the need to contribute appropriate application and dedication to the training schedules, I gave him scores, and all to no avail. The prospect of a full-time job as a swimming instructor at the end of the road, and the possibility of competitive professional swimming before that, meant nothing to him. He went to his first weekly session with the swimming club, developed a bad headache for the second and was too tired to attend the third. So ended the story of William and his talent. The only thing that mystified me was how William had learned to swim like he could without really trying in the first place. But William's talent was not the only talent discovered as a spin-off from our sporting and social activities.

One summer our ambitions got the better of us and we started some cricket-coaching classes. I was encouraged to do this by John, one of my grandsons, who was prepared to help. He was a more than useful cricketer himself. I had coached him since he was six years old and the sweat had paid off. At 17, he was opening the batting for Ampleforth College, his public school, and was in the Northants County Under-17 squad. John also played for a good local club side, the Old Northamptonians, and we were able to use their ground and nets for our sessions. So began our quest to see if we could discover and develop any hidden cricketing talent among our ranks. Amazingly, we did. Although it was apparent that the majority of our young men had never held either a cricket bat or ball in their hands, and therefore qualified for the beginners' class, we found yet again that we had on our hands an exception which proved the rule.

Jake, a new resident and at 20 an old man by our standards, claimed to have bowled in 'representative matches in the north of England', a description deemed too generic to be of any significance.

Jake had already impressed us all since arriving (but hardly in the manner he intended) with his confident views upon every conceivable subject[17] and his colourful accounts of the extraordinary events in his earlier life. For that reason, we were all taking Jake with rather hefty pinches of salt. In any case, he did not look like the fast bowler that he claimed to be. He was short and thickset rather than tall and willowy. Nevertheless, he seemed keen to join us and so, at the first net, my grandson padded up and I threw the ball to Jake. He certainly took the long run expected of a fast bowler and, as he bounded up to the wicket and let fly, I began to wonder. The first ball 'got up', as they say, sailed over John's left shoulder and hit the back of the net with a sickening thud. My eyesight is not good and so I only got a general impression of the speed of the delivery. I wondered if John had fared any better. I heard him mutter something about his crash helmet, and, as he hastily donned the protective headgear, Jake was pawing the ground on his mark with ball in hand, preparing for his second delivery. It lost nothing in comparison with the first. It was very fast, short, and again 'got up'. But this time John was ready and with some difficulty he successfully hooked the delivery off his left ear. Ten minutes later, Jake was still bounding in and John was enjoying a net session which extended him to the full.

I'm afraid there was little we could teach Jake by way of bowling. Our only hope was to improve his batting. So impressed were we with his performance with the ball that John introduced him to his club side, and Jake duly appeared and impressed on three consecutive Saturdays. Unfortunately, Jake and his cricketing talents then disappeared. One Tuesday evening when I was at the hostel for dinner, Jake asked if I would give him a character reference to help him get a 'very important job'. I explained that as I had only known him a matter of weeks the only reference I could give him was as to his prowess with a cricket ball, which presumably would not be of assistance in landing the job. Two days later he left the hostel without notice, and at the weekend the police were in attendance enquiring as to his whereabouts. Maybe the police wanted Jake to play for their police team. Or perhaps not. I never saw

---

[17] His most memorable piece of information, which he conveyed to us while we sat at dinner one evening, was that when a man ejaculates, he does so at 37.6 mph. It is not often that the non-stop noise that goes for conversation around the hostel dinner table is silenced at a stroke, but Jake's pearl of wisdom certainly did it that night.

Jake again but I (not to mention my grandson) will never forget
that first ball he bowled and the sickening thud as it hit the back
of the net. I also wondered as to the circumstances under which
Jake had learned his cricketing skills and how it seemed that he
had fallen from grace thereafter. As always, Jake's own account of
his early life was three parts imagination and one part bravado. I
never did discover the truth about his personal history.

There were other talents we found which had never previously
been exploited and which came to our notice as a result of our
various activities. Carol was a social experiment that failed, but
before that was acknowledged, and before she left us, she showed
that she possessed a most remarkable natural gift. She also had
other gifts which were less remarkable and certainly less attractive.
These were apparent from the day of her arrival and eventually
caused her downfall. In particular, she was sexually promiscuous
and sexually ignorant. As a result, she had undergone three abortions
before she reached us, aged 18. In addition, she used the most foul
and abusive language as part of her normal conversation. I served
my stint in the Army as a young man, but I had never before heard
such a stream of foul invective as came out of the mouth of this
young lady as part of her normal discourse. Altogether, not an
attractive package.

The experiment, misconceived from the outset, was to introduce
a young girl into the hostel environment to try and soften the macho
culture and encourage more considerate behaviour among our young
men. Of course, Carol was the wrong choice. Her presence in fact
offered the possibility of in-house sexual activity, and, as to the
macho behaviour and language, Carol herself led the field. She had
to go, and soon did, but not before spending some Monday evenings
with me improving her writing and reading skills. In fact, her
reading was quite good and I soon had her reading the classical
poets with genuine enthusiasm. With the blanket of foul language
discarded and replaced by the best that the English language could
provide, I suddenly became aware that this young woman had a
most beautiful contralto voice: deep, mellow and richly resonant. I
asked her if she ever did any singing, and she confirmed that she
was the star turn at the karaoke evenings held at the local pub.
The next week I brought with me a tape of recorded extracts from
the *Messiah* and asked her if she would like to do some 'proper'
singing (the term much amused her) with the Northampton Bach

Choir if I made the necessary arrangements for an introduction. She promised that she would, but only if I accompanied her. Alas, her misbehaviour in other directions had by then condemned her to an early departure from the hostel, and we were never able to launch her into 'proper' singing. The last time I saw her, she was standing at the door of her vacated room clutching a bin-bag containing her total worldly possessions. She was waiting for her social worker to collect her and take her to God knows where. Of course, she also carried with her a remarkable contralto voice, but I do not think that this would have been much help to her in the circumstances in which she found herself. I wished her well and silently prayed that somehow this talented young woman would survive.

And then there was John, our craftsman, who hid his talent from us all, fearing trespass upon his private world. John was another of my writing and reading pupils. I saw him on Friday evenings. At 23, he was older than our normal intake, but he was also a special case. He had a problem with alcohol and had been moved to Junction Road from another St Matthew's residential home where he had become unsettled. Unlike our normal boisterous intake, John was a quiet, introverted lad, small in stature and less than robust in physique. I was not surprised to learn that there had been some history of bullying during schooldays. He seemed to lack all self-confidence, particularly in social interplay with his peers. I had to wait a long time to gain his confidence, but eventually that did come. I then learned that the root cause of his problems appeared to be his inability to read, to write and to understand the basic rules of numeracy. He told me that he had always tried to keep these inadequacies to himself, and that their disclosure had led to so many embarrassing and humiliating episodes with his peers during his earlier life that he had gradually withdrawn from social contact to live the life of a loner, aided by the only thing that seemed to give him solace, namely alcohol. It was no coincidence that John's room at the hostel was the one at the end of the passage at the rear of the premises, away from the crowd.

Such was John's problem, and, although we made progress as we sweated together with the academics, it was difficult to see how our one-hour sessions could remedy the damage of the previous 20 years. What I could do, and did do, was to extend the scope of the ground we covered during our sessions, and I soon had John giving his views about the government of the day, politics and current affairs generally, the latest sporting events and even some modern history (John was fascinated by the two world wars). I am sure that John enjoyed these sessions, as I did, because he was obviously developing some measure of self-confidence in line with the progress with his basic education. We were at least facing the right direction. However, the problem with alcohol remained, and eventually it was decided that he should be removed from the hostel to undergo corrective treatment for alcoholism as recommended by the local council for addiction.

It was only when this move was imminent that John disclosed to me a personal skill that he had developed as a loner. He told me that the sole advantage to have flowed from that unfortunate status was the skill he had acquired in model-making, carefully explaining that the work and skill involved in such an activity made it of necessity a solo effort. It seemed to me from John's explanation that the freedom from social pressures while so engaged was as important as the model-making itself. But what truly amazed me was the actual model which John showed me as evidence of his skill. I had half-expected some quick-fix model aeroplane of the type often given away by the tabloid newspapers, which could be assembled in a matter of minutes. What I got, produced with an appropriate flourish by John, was a magnificent 18th-century Royal Navy man-o'-war, complete with full sails, rigging and every other imaginable detail and at least half a metre in length and height. It had apparently taken 15 months to assemble. It was indeed evidence of a rare skill and dedicated application, and I was astounded. I listened carefully again as John described how he had lovingly assembled the whole thing bit by bit, working in complete solitude hour upon hour. Of course, in the course of time, and making haste very slowly, I would have liked to have quietly introduced John to a local model-making society (and there was one) as a step towards engaging his skills in a social setting, but, alas, we did not have the time. John had kept his craft skills, his illiteracy and his problem with alcohol locked up inside himself for too long, and he duly disappeared into the system for his routine detoxification. I still visit him, but my Friday evenings are not the same without him.

I suppose, of all our activities, the one which most sustained the lads' interest, indeed passion, over the years was football. This was highlighted by our attendance at Premier League matches, where our young men could legitimately scream their heads off as devoted fans of this team or that. Residents arrived and residents left but the overall interest in football never flagged. Our visits to London and Liverpool were the highlights of our programme of events, and it was inevitable that this interest in watching football would soon develop into one of participation. If David Beckham could bend the ball, so could we. Or could we?

We put our talent to the test. We formed a six-a-side squad from residents and ex-residents and entered the local indoor leagues playing each Tuesday evening at Northampton's Danes Camp Leisure Centre. Unfortunately, our skills did not match our enthusiasm. Our playing record was abysmal. We were relegated twice in three seasons, which must be some sort of a record. Never mind, I am sure that our lads sweated a great deal of vice out of themselves in honest endeavour during our Tuesday evening sessions. What our young men lacked in football skills – which was much – they more than made up for in their explosions of energy, which were many and eventful. 'Never mind the ball, get on with the game' seemed to be their maxim. Although this practice did not win us any championship cups, it kept the lads off the streets, expended their energies (fairly) innocently and helped further the 'we' and 'us' community spirit which was so important to the hostel's continuing success. It really was a pleasure to buy them their pints of ale after each successive defeat.[18]

In addition to those recreational activities promoted, encouraged and supported by the Friends, there were, of course, other recreational activities in which our young men indulged irrespective of any Friends input. These were largely related to the use or possible abuse of alcohol, drugs and sexual activity. The St Matthew's house rules were very clear as to the position 'in-house' with regard to these matters. The rules were such that prohibition or strict control prevailed. Alcohol could only be consumed on the premises on special occasions, such as a birthday or another similar celebration, and then only with the express permission and under the strict control of the house manager. All drugs of whatever classification were expressly forbidden under any circumstances. Finally, no

---

[18] There was an interesting and pleasing sequel to our football exploits. The lady who ran the bar at the leisure centre enquired as to our charitable status and thereafter took a special interest in our abysmal football. She subsequently donated a suite of lounge furniture to us when she moved house, which we were then able to pass on to one of our ex-residents.

47

resident was allowed a visitor, male or female, to his room except with the express permission of the house manager. Compliance with these house rules virtually ensured a close control, if not the express forbidding, of all such activities on the hostel premises. No one would doubt the wisdom of such arrangements.

Outside the hostel premises, however, the house rules did not apply and the position was very different. Each young man was responsible for his own behaviour, and certainly in the early years there were more than a few residents who returned to the hostel after a weekend of indulgence or experimentation, having experienced to a greater or lesser degree alcohol inebriation, cannabis dreaminess or sexual satisfaction. Under those circumstances, the question arose as to the steps, if any, that needed to be taken by the Friends in concert with the St Matthew's staff to lay down guidelines to help our young men avoid the harmful consequences of overindulgence.

It was a difficult problem. Our young men were never tired of reminding us that they were grown men and not boys, that they knew all the facts about and inherent dangers of these adult pleasures and were thus well able to protect themselves from harmful effects. These assurances were easily given, but it was difficult not to accept them as yet another flourish of machismo, as vacuous as any of the previous flourishes. Our residents were too young to have gathered any valid long-term experience in any of these adult activities, but that did not stop them experimenting and indulging. As a result, there were some displays of objectionable drunkenness, some suspected early drug dependence and even one or two unanticipated and unwanted pregnancies. These amply illustrated both their inexperience and the worthlessness of the assurances given. So, together with St Matthew's management staff, and again acting in the capacity of dutiful but we hoped not-too-intrusive parents, we sought to advise them generally about the facts and provide them with the benefit of our own experience. To that end we enlisted the services of the local council for alcohol and drug addiction, who also took within their ambit the subject of sexual health. Various members of the council attended the hostel and gave a series of evening lectures and presentations leading to general discussion. Those dealing with alcohol and drugs were excellent as far as they went. The legal position as to the supply and consumption of alcohol and drugs was explained and a lot of factual data given, including the manner in which alcohol consumption was measured in units and how different drinks carried different units. In similar fashion, the different categories of drugs and their different effects were also explained. All this was interesting enough, but it was necessary to relate this data to the actual habits of our young men to illustrate its relevance.

Fortunately, there was one important and overriding factor limiting the indulgence of our young men in alcohol and drugs, and that was the amount of cash in their pockets. In the normal case, that was very little. In practical terms, on a weekly basis that usually meant a weekend indulgence of not more than two or three pints of beer or alternatively, a few spliffs of cannabis and maybe the popping of a big E (Ecstasy) pill.[19] It certainly would not normally include more serious indulgences, and all talk of drinking spirits and using cocaine, heroin, LSD and other highly-priced hard drugs was fanciful and nothing else. In practical terms, therefore, we were content if our young men could restrict their weekend appetites to a beer/cannabis diet. In this manner, we would hope to avoid the particular difficulty and inherent danger of progression from soft to hard drugs. Our young men were well aware that unlike alcohol, which has much the same effect whether taken through beers, wines or spirits, different drugs had very different effects, ranging from restful relaxation through 'highs' and 'lows' to hallucinations. To the young user of cannabis (and most were), the temptation was to sample one of the harder drugs to experience the new 'buzz'. It is that progression that can of course lead to addiction, and that was the message that we constantly preached. One has to say, however, that our preaching was materially assisted by the impecuniousness of our young men. But one unfortunate exception comes to mind. One lad smoked cannabis spliffs at the weekend. At a party, he was introduced to amphetamines ('speed' or 'whiz'). As our young man was soon to find out, unlike cannabis, which relaxes, soothes and produces a state of contentment, speed produces a 'high' of excitement and exhilaration where everything appears possible. Although the 'high' is followed by the inevitable 'low', our young man became hooked on speed. He turned to burglary to feed the cost of what

---

[19] There was one complication. The giro cheques in payment of social-security benefits were issued on a fortnightly basis. Double money was therefore in their pockets at least every other weekend, but even so the cash was insufficient to fund the purchase of hard drugs.

49

became his addiction. He ended up in Woodhill maximum-security prison.[20]

The position with sexual activity was very different. There was no constraint as to cost. Our young men and their female friends were therefore literally free to indulge – and they did. Both in the general and the particular, they were sexually promiscuous. They formed and dissolved sexual relationships as it pleased them. There was no need for the employment and payment of prostitutes, but as in those relationships there was no need for any deep emotional input between the consenting parties. The only constraint arose in the rather exceptional case where a lad was a virgin and inexperienced in sexual activity. Under the influence of his peer group this was soon remedied. Again, it was a feature of the macho image to be seen as some sort of sexual athlete, and although talk tended to boost the image the overall picture was certainly one of vigorous promiscuity and experimentation. Our young charges seemed to view sexual activity as an extension of the entertainment industry, for which no payment was demanded, as was first explained to me by Pip Bailey. There was no question of any moral issue. Even their attitude, or non-attitude, to the conventional caveats and wisdom issued by the secular authorities in connection with sexual health, was irresponsible to the point of recklessness. There was as much chance of getting them to wear a condom as there was a bowler hat or a pair of long johns. It was the macho thing again. They saw no reason why they should cloak their pride and joy under a cowl or deposit their seed in a little rubber bag. In their minds, responsibility for frustrating the natural consequences of the act lay fairly and squarely with their female partner, who was expected to be 'on the pill'. Unwanted pregnancies therefore hardly came into the reckoning any more than the transfer of disease did. These were things that only happened to other people – until, of course, it happened to them. As a result of this feckless attitude we found ourselves advising more than one young man over the years to visit the genito-urinary clinic at the local hospital.[21]

We turned again for help to the local council for addiction, which

---

[20] I used to visit him. On one such visit he gave a compelling explanation of his own plight and that of his fellow inmates when he said, 'Smithy, if there was no booze and no drugs, this place would be empty.' It was this sort of message that we were constantly plugging to our residents.

[21] Chlamydia and gonorrhoea were the most common infections.

included sexual health in its remit but their response was disappointing. Once again they visited the hostel and ran through their normal course of lectures and presentations. They gave us the facts about male and female sexual physiology and how in union they interacted under normal circumstances to produce a new life. They also gave us the facts (which included quite frightening statistics) as to the growth and nature of the sexual diseases and their transmission by intercourse. These two topics then led on inevitably to the subject of the condóm, which was described by one enthusiastic lecturer as the one item which could effectively frustrate the natural outcome of intercourse and thus ensure that sexual activity could be 'uninhibited fun'. I am not sure as to what effect this exposition on the mechanics of sex, and how the workings could be frustrated so as to preserve the pleasures but not the consequences of the act itself, had upon our audience of young men. I doubt that they were any more uplifted than I was. I also doubted that their attitudes or non-attitudes changed thereafter. It was an unresolved problem.[22]

By way of a postscript, there is an interesting theory that might explain why our young men rose like the proverbial salmon at the prospect of sexual adventure. It is brought to mind by the particular circumstances of one of our young men, Hugh, aged 17, who was the subject of an extraordinary charge from an enraged husband that the young lad had seduced his wife. Hugh was one of our new residents at the time. He was on that account quieter, more sober and more withdrawn than our other residents, and I know that he had received some stick for his apparent sexual naivety. Having met both the 'seduced' wife and the enraged husband, I was quite confident as to who had seduced whom, and particularly so when I discussed the matter with Hugh. The details are unimportant, but Hugh's remarks in explanation certainly bear repeating. He told me that he had been babysitting for the mother. According to Hugh, on returning home, minus the husband, she had sat down on the

---

[22] A problem fully reflected in the frightening national statistics relating to unwanted pregnancies, abortions and the incidence of sexual disease among young people. Our lads were not ignorant as to the physiological facts. These had been pumped into them from their early teens either by formal 'sex education' at school or via information from their peer group. The fundamental flaw was that as a result, they were experimenting in an adult activity – with all its emotional, psychological and moral ramifications as well as the physiological ones – and their adolescent minds could not cope. They were bound to make mistakes – and did. The fault lay not with them but with a social system that seemed to promote this disharmony and yet failed to recognise its fundamental flaw.

settee where Hugh was sitting, had put her arms around him and had begun to cuddle him. Hugh's next words astounded me. 'Smithy,' he said, 'no one had ever cuddled me before in my whole life and I just wanted to do the same to her, I couldn't help myself.' I could hardly believe what I was hearing. How had Hugh's parents expressed their love for him in early life? Or had they ever done so? I did not doubt the truth of Hugh's remarks, though at first I thought him to be a case on his own. But was he? Had similar circumstances prevailed in the case of our other young men? Was perhaps the reason why they responded so readily to the stimuli provided through the intimacies, the tenderness, the touching and the emotional input (even where manufactured for the occasion) which normally constitutes an overture to lovemaking simply because they had been starved of affection and demonstrable love in their early lives? Fact or fiction? Only the lads knew, but it was certainly the case with Hugh. He had been 17 years without a cuddle. Was it any wonder that he felt unwanted and unloved and was it any wonder that he should be ready for the sucker punch from the first person who offered?

The times, events, anecdotes and characters that I have so described in this chapter comprise but a snapshot of the whole picture of hostel life during my near ten-year tenure. I am sure to have omitted many items that have now slipped from my addled and disintegrating memory and for that I apologise to all those legions of young men who have escaped specific mention in my narrative. I know they will see themselves as an essential part of the generality of my remarks.

Chapter Four

Mick the Lad – or Michael the Student?

'All experience is an arch to build upon.'
Henry Brooks Adams (1907)

I always had great difficulty in spelling Michael Crague's name. Almost as much as I had in trying to keep him on the road to rehabilitation. In the end I mastered my spelling difficulties, but if I record a win on the rehabilitation front, I am not, I think, giving divine providence its due. Mick was one of our early residents, and I always bracket him in my thoughts with his fellow resident, friend and rival, Pat Miller. They were great rivals for the post of pack leader at the hostel, being a few years older than the other residents. When both were consigned to Woodhill Prison at Milton Keynes a few years later, they resumed their friendship and rivalry there. Never mind the ball or the circumstances, get on with the game.

I first met Mick as a new resident at one of our early barbecues, which were our equivalent of the Buckingham Palace garden party. The function was held in the back garden of the hostel, and friends, benefactors and useful contacts from the great bureaucracies in the sky (the social services, etc.) were invited to attend. The residents, all dressed up in their best bibs and tuckers, were duly paraded as waiters, ushers and general attendants. All were under strict instruction to watch their language, invest in some genteel behaviour and learn some of the arts of civilised social intercourse. That was the theory anyway, but in fact the proceedings that afternoon passed off quite famously even if the clouds of blue smoke from the charcoal furnace enveloped all and sundry from time to time. The sun shone, the chatter was ceaseless and much good was done in more ways than one. There was something rather endearing about seeing our teenage tearaways chatting with our benefactors, some of whom were the wrong side of eighty. They did it very well too.

None better than Michael Crague, who was there with his girlfriend at the time, Celia. On being introduced and talking to Mick's escort, I learned that her father was a very great friend of an old and much respected ex-client of mine. My interest in Mick was thus stimulated and more so when I had an opportunity of talking to him too. He was tall, dark and, if not handsome, he ran very close to it. But the most conspicuous feature, which was so noticeable in what, after all, was the rough end of institutional life, was that he had somehow and somewhere acquired what I could only describe as a polished veneer to both his conversation and behaviour. I remember thinking that such a protective shield would have served him well in company far removed from and much more sophisticated than what prevailed at Junction Road. That it was a veneer to fit the circumstances of the afternoon I had no doubt,[1] but the fact that it was an available extra in Mick's bag of tools heightened my interest in this young man and the prospects for his future. I was also reminded of that rather uncomfortable feeling that I had experienced when I first had words with young Freddy, one of our first-ever residents. As with Freddy, so with Mick. Given half a chance, I felt that Mick could buy and sell me ten times over before I became aware of what was going on. I used to think of Freddy as 'Mr Big'. If Mick had arrived at the hostel at the same time as Freddy, there would have been two Mr Bigs. That would have been interesting. Here was another young man steeped in street experience and street wisdom. The facts I obtained subsequently about Mick did not belie my judgement.

Mick's background and personal history like so many of our young men were horrific. The product of a one-night stand, his mother had only met his father on that single occasion. He had never been seen again from that day to this. Eventually, the inevitable stepfather and half-sister had appeared to make up the hybrid family. According to Mick's grandmother Margaret, a dear old lady who I

---

[1] I was wrong. It was an inherited characteristic, not a veneer. See later.

54

got to know very well and who had remained loyal and supportive to Mick throughout his chequered career, Mick was almost shunned by the 'new' family and relegated to the position of an outsider. In which position, according to Margaret, he was constantly humiliated and bullied by his stepfather. The result was inevitable. As a ten-year-old, Mick became an unmanageable rebel and was taken into care. At 13, he ran away from his care home and for the next four years lived on the streets of London before he was found and brought back to Northampton, where he joined us at Junction Road.

Everything he had ever learned, he had learned on the street (and at whose knee?). Although his formal education appears to have been sparse to the point of non-existence up to early teenage, it had certainly been next to nil thereafter. Nevertheless, I soon found that Mick could in fact read and write fluently and could also cope with numeracy well beyond an elementary level. How or where he had acquired these skills I have no idea, but when asked to write on a particular topic he would demonstrate yet again as with so many of our undereducated lads that there was an inherent if undeveloped intelligence crying out for proper expression. If that was added to his outgoing personality and polish, his leadership qualities as illustrated in the acceptance of the position as pack leader by the other residents at the time, then taken as a whole, those were qualities which ought to lead to a very worthwhile career. It was also not difficult to read the direction that career ought to take. Michael knew the street like the back of his hand and he knew all about the sort of people that lived on the street and the problems they had. Who better than Mick in terms of experience and practical knowledge to become a social worker in the difficult field of youth work among the homeless, a world he knew so well, providing of course that he kept his own nose clean? There was, of course, another mountain to climb if that dream was ever to become a reality. To do the job properly, Mick would have to cope with a certain amount of academic study, which would be completely new territory to him. If he was to aspire to any post other than the most junior then he would need to aim for a diploma in sociology. That was not the most prestigious or the most difficult academic hurdle to get over, but Mick would have to cover a lot of ground. Would he have the mental toughness to take it on? Was it to be a continuation of Mick the Lad as now, or was it to be Michael the Student?

Before I even had a chance to put my thoughts to Mick, there was an unwelcome intervention that immediately reduced such thoughts to pure theory. There was not much that Mick had not experienced on the streets of London,[2] and experimentation with both soft and hard drugs had been on the list. When he was taken in at Junction Road, due warning was given that all drugs, hard and soft, were strictly forbidden on the premises and any infringement would bring about immediate expulsion.[3] I can recall an occasion shortly after Mick joined us when I took the lads to the local indoor bowling alley. Mick behaved like a demented thing, quite out of character, and he was obviously 'high' on something a bit stronger than Coca-Cola.[4] I reported my misgivings on returning to the hostel and had words with Mick the next day. But perhaps almost inevitably, Mick was soon after caught bringing drugs into the hostel and was accordingly and rightfully expelled. I was bitterly disappointed but had learned to accept disappointment as part and parcel of our endeavours at Junction Road.

Mick's expulsion should, of course, have ended my relationship with him, but it did not. A chance (or divinely inspired?) meeting with him a few weeks later on a Northampton street changed all that. It was a Wednesday morning and I had just ended my usual Wednesday morning stint at the kitchen in Ash Street. I was driving away from my parking space when I noticed Mick on the other side of the street. I hardly recognised him. I stopped the car, crossed the street and joined him. He did not recognise me. He was clearly 'stoned', was unkempt and dirty, and his face, devoid of all colour, was covered with sores. I offered him a lift but he did not seem to know where he was going. I gave him some money and told him to go to the kitchen, which was only just around the corner. There he could get something to eat and drink, I told him, but when I left he made off in the opposite direction. I was shocked by what I had seen. I had no idea that drug addiction could ravage

---

[2] I remember him showing me how to open my own locked car without breaking the lock and telling me how he regularly slept in the rear seat of parked cars. One morning, the owner/driver started the car and moved off with Mick still under a rug in the well of the back seat. He got out at the first traffic lights.

[3] The use of drugs, consumption of alcohol and sexual activity away from the hostel premises were not in themselves grounds for expulsion but were certainly items that were regularly discussed and for which advice was given. It was only on the premises that these activities were strictly forbidden.

[4] It was amphetamines or 'speed'.

the body and brain to the extent that I had just witnessed. Nevertheless, I felt impelled to regain contact with Mick and get him at least to see the drug-addiction people with whom we had contacts. I was too late. I found out that Mick had been literally 'on the run' when I had met him and was wanted for alleged burglary offences.[5]

The next time I saw Mick was in the Crown Court in Northampton. I sat at the rear of the Court. Mick was in the dock. The case against him was straightforward and he pleaded guilty to the offences as charged. The most alarming feature was the recital of previous offences going back to his days in London. He was obviously going to be sent down – and was. He was dispatched for an 18-month sentence to the young offenders institution at Glen Parva, near Leicester. I remember thinking that his nine months' incarceration (he might reasonably expect a nine months' remission for good behaviour) might at least make some contribution towards rehabilitation from what was obviously an addiction to drugs. Fortunately, there was another plus factor that arose out of the depressing proceedings at the Crown Court, for it was there that I first met Margaret, Mick's grandmother.

I had noticed that there was another spectator to the proceedings, who had wept copiously when the list of previous offences was being read out. She was an elderly lady who seemed to have stepped out of a previous century, such was her garb and genteel deportment. As I introduced myself to her, and she to me, I suddenly realised where Mick's polish came from. It was an inherited characteristic, and I knew now that it went back at least two generations. Margaret seemed anxious to talk and we therefore lingered for some time in the reception area. I was soon fully acquainted with Mick's early history, which had led to his running away to London. Margaret was obviously very fond of Mick and bitter about the manner in which she said her own daughter and husband had sidelined and neglected young Mick by treating him almost as an outsider. She told me that she had personally done what she could to give young Mick the love and care which he had failed to find within his own home. She also related with enthusiasm what a bright and intelligent young boy Mick had been in the early days. This did not surprise me, as most of what she told me was confirmed by the official

---

[5] There is, of course, a close correlation between burglaries and drug addiction. The addiction has to be fed and funded.

record. Nevertheless, I carefully stored away in my mind everything she had said. I told her that I would be pleased to escort her to Glen Parva as soon as we were allowed to visit. So began a period of regular visits with Margaret to the special institution near Leicester which catered exclusively for the needs of young offenders. And joining the both of us when her other activities allowed was Rose, who had been in charge of the hostel when Mick was there, and had the painful duty of expelling him. She had since departed and gone on to higher and better things at the much larger YMCA hostel in Northampton. Rose was and always had been very fond of Mick, knew about his family background, or lack of it, and knew Mick as well as anyone. Like Margaret and I, she believed there was a lot of good in Mick. I am sure that the three of us, and the regular visiting and correspondence that we were able to sustain, communicated to Mick that there was solid support available to him, although it still apparently remained very thin on the ground as far as his immediate family was concerned.

My visits to Glen Parva in connection with Mick's enforced stay there were the first occasions that I had of acquainting myself with HM prisons. I had subsequent occasions to visit other prisons and young offender institutions at Onley, near Rugby, at Woodhill in Milton Keynes and Bullington near Henley-on-Thames as our young men took up residence in these places from time to time. As a result of my various visits I came firmly to the conclusion that if it was as difficult for the inmates to get out of these establishments as it was for us to get into them, then it was no wonder that jailbreaks were few and far between.

Glen Parva was typical. Armed with fistfuls of paperwork by way of permits, proof of identity and particulars of the proposed visit, we first of all entered a reception block – a world of interlocking but connected chambers – where we were interrogated,[6] searched, partially disrobed, passed through x-ray machines and subjected to the antics of sniffer dogs intent upon pulling our trousers down to disclose the bundles of crack cocaine stuffed in our underwear. All this as we were driven like a flock of sheep through the interlocking doors and chambers under the watchful eyes of the attendant prison

---

[6] Tired of the everlasting and repetitive interrogations and tired of describing myself as a retired chartered accountant (for which I had no proof), I once described myself at Woodhill as a retired bank robber (for which I also held no proof). Fortunately, the prison officer, who knew me well as a regular visitor, merely smiled and noted down 'retired chartered accountant'.

officers. Eventually, in a rather dishevelled state and with more than a degree of irritability, we reached the actual visiting room.

The inmates, clad in their distinctive coloured bibs, were always already seated at their respective numbered positions on a long bench that provided an effective segregation between each young prisoner and his visitors. I always found the visits profoundly depressing while at the same time trying to project an upbeat attitude for the benefit of Mick and those others that I visited over the course of the next few years. That young men on the very threshold of their lives, with so much to work for and aspire to, should be locked away in a thoroughly negative environment devoid of all personal privacy and dignity seemed to me barbaric, especially where, as was the case with Mick, the crime did not include any element of injury to a person other than himself. Mick himself always laid the blame at the door of drugs and alcohol, saying that if these 'crutches' (his word) were not available, penal institutions like Glen Parva would be empty. I thought that was begging the question. If crutches were needed why were they needed? What was the disability that led to the need for crutches? On reflection, was it any wonder that Mick had succumbed to drugs, having regard to the sort of home life he should have had as a youngster and never got?

But these somewhat abstract thoughts were not of immediate priority during our visits to Glen Parva. The priority then was to try and ensure that Mick did not throw in the sponge and settle for the life of a petty criminal and a graduation fired by hopelessness towards professional criminality leading to God knows where. Mick himself gave nothing away. Although it was his first stretch behind bars, he served his time without particular incident and with no hiccups for bad behaviour. He readily accepted – indeed seemed enthusiastic about – our suggestions as to a possible future career involving the care of young offenders, and he also accepted and was grateful for our promised support in that undertaking. It was also put to him that all these long-term plans were worthless unless he could kick the drug habit, and we emphasised that only he could ride that particular horse.

In the meantime, on his release from Glen Parva we would do what we could to find him accommodation and a post of employment. In the event I found that the one was easier than the other. A small flat was found on advantageous terms through a charitable trust, and housing benefit through the social services was applied for and obtained. So far so good, but then our luck seemed to run out as doors were firmly slammed in our faces as far as a job was concerned. As soon as mention was made of Mick's spell at Glen Parva, one prospect after another quickly collapsed. In one case, there was a particular cause for disappointment and some bitterness. Before his entanglement with drugs, and while resident at the hostel, Mick had held down a job as junior salesman with B&Q, the prominent DIY suppliers. He had done very well there, earning good money including bonuses, and had never given cause for complaint. Application for a job was therefore made to B&Q as a first priority after his release from prison. It was refused point blank. According to the store manager, his previous boss, company regulations barred his further employment because of his criminal record. I wrote at length to the B&Q area manager, explaining all the circumstances of Mick's fall from grace and pointing out that the relevant offences were nearly two years old and that Mick was now 'dry'. All to no avail. The B&Q bar to employment was typical. Company regulations barring the employment of those with criminal records were quoted over and over again. It seemed that all and sundry were intent upon collapsing the umbrella when it rained the hardest.[7]

In the meantime, another umbrella had also collapsed. Celia, Mick's girlfriend, who I had met at our barbecue, had departed for pastures new during Mick's incarceration. I did not lose too much sleep about this loss because I knew that Mick would very soon remedy that position after his release. In fact, within the space of ten days he had a new lady love clambering all over him. Nevertheless, I pondered for a while as to the apparent fickleness of the young. It seemed to me that desertion at a time of need had again been well illustrated. It was all very well for old fogies like Mick's grandmother and I (I hesitate to describe Rose in similar terms) to take an interest and lend support by visits and correspondence, but similar support from a loyal girlfriend would have been invaluable. Was that asking too much from the younger generation?

The unsuccessful hunt for paid employment gradually became a major problem after Mick's release. In the end, it was the main

---

[7] I am constantly reminded of the 'company regulations' of B&Q when I witness its incessant advertising campaign leading up to Christmas, the season of goodwill and compassion.

factor which helped bring about another major setback to Mick's rehabilitation. By the time of his release he was 20 years old. He had no particular skills or education, but he did have a criminal record. He certainly made applications for jobs, lots of them in every conceivable human activity, and attended countless unsuccessful interviews. Rose and I supplied him with any number of references revealing the facts surrounding his criminal record and our views as to the circumstances which had prompted such a record. In almost every case, as with B&Q, those dealing with Mick's applications hid behind their 'company regulations' barring employment to those with criminal records. I certainly gained the impression that the so-called company regulations were being manufactured on the hoof to save the interviewing officer from personal embarrassment.

As time went on Mick, of course, became depressed and began to lose hope. Most of his old friends and colleagues were making their way slowly, if not all that surely, up their respective career ladders and beginning to earn real money. Meanwhile Mick was living on social-security handouts in subsidised accommodation at the very lowest end of the scale. Of course, such a state of affairs could not continue and did not. Mick had rather extravagant habits and they required funding from cash in his pocket. He was not called Mick the Lad for nothing. Within the year he was back in prison and this time it was not a young offenders' institution, where the regimes are reckoned to be tailored to some extent to fit the particular circumstances applicable to youngsters.[8] This time it was the real thing and Mick was swallowed up into the bowels of Woodhill maximum-security prison at Milton Keynes. The offences which landed him there were again housebreaking and burglary. Years afterwards, I asked Mick the obvious question, 'Why again?' His answer was as simple as it was truthful. 'My friends had money. I had none. I therefore turned my efforts to the only thing that I was good at, which was burglary.'

I had tried earlier, when I appeared as a character witness at Mick's Crown Court trial, to convey the near inevitability of Mick's further offending by reason of the circumstances I have just described and in particular the difficulty in obtaining employment. I spoke

---

[8] None of our residents who were so incarcerated ever identified the special benefits applicable. Maybe it was two to a single cell instead of three.

about his life at the hostel and the qualities that he had displayed there. I also mentioned what I thought should be a factor to be taken into account when sentencing him, and that was the serious application he had made to theoretical study. Ever since his release from Glen Parva he had visited my flat each Tuesday evening, where I had introduced him to a variety of academic subjects. Margaret and I knew that if our long-term plans for Mick worked out then he would have to do some academic study towards gaining a diploma or, who knows, perhaps even a degree in sociology. I was therefore anxious to test the temperature of the water and ascertain if Mick had both the interest and the ability to take up serious academic work. After one or two sessions (I remember the Industrial Revolution and the elements of corporate law as particular topics), I realised that I was introducing a duck to water. All the latent intelligence came to the surface and fused with an honest-to-goodness enthusiasm. The brew was quite intoxicating. I doubt that the presiding judge at the Crown Court proceedings was similarly intoxicated by what I had said as to Mick's potential, but when passing sentence he did at least make the point that educational facilities would be available at whichever penal establishment Mick attended, and he hoped that Mick would take advantage of them. As far as the learned judge was concerned, Mick had chosen a life of crime as a way out of his difficulties and he had to pay the price for that decision. All of which was very true and very depressing.

I next saw Mick when Margaret and I made our first visit to HM prison at Woodhill in Milton Keynes. The procedures for entry into that establishment were very similar and as complicated as they had been at Glen Parva, but we were getting used to being treated with our fellow visitors like a flock of sheep and having dogs sniffing up our trouser legs searching for the bags of cocaine we brought in strapped to our genitals. I found this regular procedure particularly nauseating, not so much for myself as for the 80-year-old female companion at my side. It seemed that personal dignity was the first thing that was jettisoned on entering these establishments. At Woodhill, unlike Glen Parva, there was an extensive yard separating the reception buildings from the prison block proper, where the actual visiting area was situated. This again was very similar to what we had already seen, though on a much bigger scale. Negotiating the yard involved a slight gradient and more than a few steps. I noticed during the course of our successive visits that Margaret was finding it increasingly difficult to negotiate this obstacle course, and when I asked she informed me that she was unwell and 'under the doctor'. I later found out that she was in fact suffering from an inoperable cancer. It was painful and it was messy. Nevertheless, this quite remarkable woman, then over 80 years of age and literally dying on her feet, insisted on accompanying me on every visit I made to Woodhill until she ran the full course and her death intervened. During these visits she would never tire of recounting endless anecdotes of Mick's early life and how she had tried to give him the love and affection that she felt was so lacking in his own home. She obviously loved Mick deeply, and the misdemeanours that had blighted his young life, to which others might draw attention, in no way affected that love. She once said to me, 'When you love someone, you just love them. You don't assess them.' She was a remarkable woman, full of loyalty and love. I just hoped that other parts of her, as well as the polish, had worn off on Mick. I realised it was for her sake, as well as for Mick's and my own, that I felt obligated to keep going with Mick's rehabilitation, even though our subject was now buried in the bowels of a maximum-security prison.

Mick seemed well able to cope with life at Woodhill, although he later admitted to finding the regime harsher than at Glen Parva. He was now mixing with hardened criminals, most of whom were reoffenders. None knew that better than the prison officers charged with their safekeeping. There was more talk of security and less of rehabilitation. I was anxious that Mick should continue some sort of academic activity if at all possible at Woodhill, having made such a good start with me. With that in mind I requested an interview with the education officer, which eventually I obtained. Although the official paid lip service to my suggestions and eventually arranged an introductory course in sociology through the Open University (which Mick welcomed and worked at with enthusiasm in a most difficult environment), it was apparent that Mr Blair's clarion call for 'education, education, education' had not reached the confines of Woodhill Prison. The inmates were of all ages, and most of them had long since given up the idea that education was the answer to all their prayers. Unfortunately, that seemed to be the view shared and encouraged by the prison officers too. Such was the environment in which we hoped that Mick would study.

Mick himself seemed generally well able to take care of himself. After all, he had done that since his early teenage years in all sorts of circumstances. He seemed to accept imprisonment as one of the occupational hazards of his profession, which was burglary. It was an attitude which thoroughly alarmed me, being indicative of a possible lurch towards a future of serious criminality. I did everything in my correspondence with and visits to Mick to eradicate that tendency. I constantly talked up the possibilities for the future. I told him that in collusion with Rose his old friend, and Georgina, her replacement as the hostel manager at Junction Road, I had prepared and agreed a detailed plan for his employment and living accommodation following his release. Meanwhile, Mick kept his head well down at Woodhill and, subject to one hiccup, stayed out of trouble. The one hiccup during his two-year stay well illustrated that if there are any level playing fields about, none of them have got as far as Woodhill Prison. The incident made me much more angry than Mick, and culminated in my writing directly to HM Inspectorate of Prisons, who were sympathetic and yet sublimely ineffective.

Mick had always been an inveterate gambler, albeit for relatively small stakes, and soon after he arrived at Woodhill he set up a weekly football pool. Having secured the position of junior librarian,[9] and thereby the use of a copying machine, he was well able to handle the weekly administration of what was an enjoyable yet relatively harmless activity. Like topsy, it grew and grew by dint of its own success and at least three prison officers were included among the clientele. Inevitably, the scheme became known to the Woodhill hierarchy, who decided that it broke practically every rule in the book. There was an immediate internal (of course) inquiry. As a result, Mick lost all the privileges that he had earned for good behaviour (including his post as librarian) while the three prison officers who were regular weekly participators in the scheme carefully and consistently denied all knowledge of it, let alone their participation in it. I was incensed by the dishonesty and the closing of the Establishment ranks. Mick said he could produce a dozen or more inmates who would confirm the involvement of the prison officers, but he was also the experienced professional who knew only too

---

[9] How he obtained the position, only Mick knows. It was one of the cushiest numbers in the whole establishment.

well the ways of a wicked world unknown to me. He rightly considered that dishonesty was par for the course and that we would get absolutely nowhere with any form of official complaint. Mick's downgrading did not last but it certainly brought to an end the football-pool activity. As at Glen Parva, Mick's ability to cope with prison life like a professional, although worrying in one sense, at least ensured that he was free from drugs over an extended period of time, and, hopefully, was using that time to give serious thought to his future. Certainly, we hoped that our constant correspondence and regular visits bolstered and encouraged that position.

Unfortunately, and at the same time, I was able to view at close quarters the case of a young man I knew well who was almost broken, both physically and mentally, by a term of imprisonment at Woodhill which coincided with Mick's. Pat Miller, Mick's friend and rival at the hostel when both were still teenagers, was serving a sentence for arson. While still at the hostel, his girlfriend Jill had become pregnant. As a result Pat had left the hostel and together with his girlfriend had started to live independently, although they were in no financial position to do so. Pat had no particular skills and could hardly read or write. There was also little help from the respective families. Although Pat had taken two jobs to help balance the domestic budget, working as a labourer on building sites during the day and as a club doorman in the evening, the young couple had fallen into arrears with the payment of their bills, and at the time when the baby was due to arrive they were facing eviction. Pat was then offered the sum of £500 in cash if he would 'do a job' for one of the connections he had acquired through his work as a club doorman. The 'job' was to set fire to a small empty factory at night-time for reasons known only to the person who had employed Pat to do it.

Pat's thoughts never got further than the £500, which would square up all his bills and give him and his family a new start. Of course, the story ended at the Crown Court and Woodhill Prison rather than at any celebratory party for the squaring of debts. Pat was in no way a master arsonist and never acted like one in carrying out his task. He was an easy pickup for the police, and Mick and Pat were accordingly reunited, albeit in an unwelcome environment. But their respective performances at Woodhill were so different. Mick showed just how tough and robust he was under his polished exterior, whereas Pat collapsed both physically and mentally under the pressure of a harsh environment. He had never been all that robust under his macho exterior and was plainly physically afraid of his fellow inmates. This was soon picked up by the hard men of the prison. As a result he was severely bullied and humiliated. He lost whatever appetite he had and so lost weight steadily until he was little more than skin and bone. On entry into Woodhill he weighed in at a fraction over twelve stone. Within two months he was down to less than ten stone, a fact which appears to have escaped the notice of the prison authorities. It was only when he attempted to slash his wrists that proper medical and psychological care was made available, and he was moved first of all into the sickbay and then into the 'self-harm' wing, away from his tormentors. It was not possible for Mick to help or offer any comfort to his old friend, because he was housed on a different wing of the prison and was not even allowed to visit Pat in sickbay.

When I became aware of the situation, I began to pick up Pat's girlfriend when Margaret and I were visiting Mick so that she could visit Pat at the same time. I also started to write regularly to Pat in the same upbeat mood that I used in Mick's letters, although in Pat's case I was obliged to use the simplest of phrasing. Eventually Pat did make a partial recovery, at least in physical terms, and was released early. On reflection, it is apparent that sending a young man hardly out of his teens to be bullied by hardened criminals in a high-security prison, and for a first offence, was a decision of particular idiocy, even barbarism. I don't think Pat Miller will ever forget the experience and I don't suppose that the learned judge who sent him to Woodhill will ever learn about Pat Miller's experience. That is a great pity.

During the latter part of Mick's time at Woodhill, his grandmother Margaret became very ill and it was obvious that she did not have long to live. Eventually, she was taken into Northampton General Hospital and I wrote to Mick explaining the position. He applied immediately for a compassionate visit to the hospital and, after we had supplied the necessary medical evidence, the application was granted. The visit was arranged for a midweek afternoon and on that day I hastened to Margaret to tell her that Mick was on his way to see her. She was delighted and made special arrangements to have her hair done to mark the occasion. I remember thinking, 'polished to the end'. Although in considerable pain in spite of constant doses of pain-relieving drugs, Margaret was still mentally very much with it, even if physically very weak. When Mick arrived I prepared to withdraw from the bedside, but both Mick and Margaret asked me to stay on. Mick was handcuffed to a prison officer and I expected both the handcuffs and the prison officer would disappear once the screens were pulled around Margaret's bed, but that was not the case. During the last conversation that Mick ever had with his dying grandmother, the one person who had been a constant support throughout his life, he sat at her bedside manacled to a prison officer who was thus a party to every word that passed between them. Mick wept, as well he might. In my naivety I had expected the handcuffs to be removed before entry into what was, after all, a public ward, and I can only guess as to the embarrassment for Mick when that turned out not to be the case.

If the deathbed scene with the prison officer in close attendance defies belief, there was a repeat performance when poor Margaret died a week or so later. Mick was again allowed compassionate leave for the funeral and again attended the proceedings at the local crematorium duly manacled to a prison officer throughout. This time, there was more than a look of embarrassment on Mick's face. There was a look of intense grief. I thought that on this occasion in particular Mick was truly mindful of the great loss he had suffered and of how much he owed to a dear old lady who, unlike so many, had never given up on him. So had ended the life of this gracious lady. She had prayed constantly for Mick's rehabilitation but had never lived to see it.

This time, when Mick was released from Woodhill prison, we were better prepared. During his absence Rose, Georgie and I had put our heads together and we now had a grand scheme awaiting him to take care of the twin problems of accommodation and a job. At least, the good Lord would award us maximum points for trying. Georgie was to provide accommodation for Mick at the hostel. The upstairs flat had been originally intended for an assistant to the manager and it was in that capacity, albeit on a part-time basis, that Mick was to move in. In return for his services as assistant to Georgie, Mick would live rent-free. He would also be provided with sufficient time off to pursue his academic studies. Mick was by this time some four or five years older than any of the residents at the hostel and knew the street, whence most of the youngsters came, like the back of his hand. No one had a better practical background for handling the youngsters, and the St Matthew's

Society (unlike B&Q and others with their company regulations), in their wisdom and compassion, were prepared to back the experiment, which represented Mick's first steps by way of an apprenticeship in social service with the emphasis on youth work. He would learn much from Georgie about administrative tasks, interviewing techniques, shopping and cooking for nine or ten hungry mouths and so on. At the same time, by helping Georgie generally, he would discharge his commitment as to rent and hopefully make progress with his academic studies. In addition to this provision for accommodation, we, or rather Rose, agreed to provide Mick with the opportunity of earning real money by working part-time as one of her assistants at the YMCA hostel, which was only a few hundred yards from Junction Road. Rose was employed as a general manager at that establishment and it was within her authority to appoint part-time helpers. Certainly, Mick's duties at Junction Road would not occupy all his time and we all considered that an opportunity to cash in on some real earnings was important, having regard to what had happened when Mick was released from Glen Parva. It was important to put cash from earnings in Mick's pocket. There was of course another point of importance. During the course of his daily duties he would come under the surveillance of both Rose and Georgie. He was free of drugs when he left Woodhill and I knew that Rose and Georgie would do all that they could to keep it that way.

All these aspects of the Grand Scheme were put to Mick before he was released from Woodhill and he readily agreed to the suggestions. Actually, a better description would perhaps be that he enthusiastically agreed with certain of our suggestions but was lukewarm about his ability to deliver on all fronts at one and the same time. Nevertheless, he was grateful for our efforts on his behalf and was prepared to give the scheme a run and see how things worked out. He certainly started off firing on all cylinders when he eventually left Woodhill. He settled in well at Junction Road and was a great help to Georgie. Surprisingly, he mastered the intricacies of bookkeeping so quickly that Georgie soon left the weekly 'balancing up' hurdle exclusively to Mick. He was also extremely able in sorting out personal problems man to man with the youngsters, with whom he established an older–younger brother relationship. He organised and ran a five-a-side indoor soccer team, which he recruited from residents and ex-residents. Even if not topping the tables in terms of performance and skills, it certainly helped promote a lot of fun and community spirit. He also organised various trips by way of treats for the residents – I remember a trip to Alton Towers Theme Park which was the highlight of the summer.

As agreed, he also continued his academic studies, and I saw him on a weekly basis to offer encouragement. Mick did not find solitary study easy, but the addition of a personal tutor and the discussion which invariably followed showed only too clearly how his mind could be stimulated into one worthy of the very best of coaching, such was his raw intelligence. I used to tell Mick that his brain was like a giant rice pudding which needed a good stir with a big stick to get it into overdrive. But once there, it was worth it.

But the plain fact which became very apparent as the early weeks and months passed by was that the authors of the grand scheme for Mick's rehabilitation – and none more than I – were perhaps more enthusiastic than the intended beneficiary. We had greatly underestimated the psychological leap required to go from a lifetime of criminality to a new life of responsible mainstream living. We should have been making haste much more slowly, allowing Mick to take his own time to make the radical readjustment necessary. The immediate targets were too ambitious when taken together, and Mick being Mick he became selective with his targets. It soon became apparent that Mick's abiding interest and enthusiasm was centred upon the earning of ready money and what he could do with it, not in the dim and distant future with the aid of academic qualification but rather in the here and now, today and tomorrow. Mick was a great socialiser and an elegant dresser much taken with his personal appearance, and he was never happier than when indulging these appetites to the full. For this reason, he was quite willing, indeed anxious, to work each and every night at the YMCA if it would bring cash to his pocket, which it did. The worrying thing was that the spending rate was equal to and then in excess of the earnings rate. As a result, financial problems arose. I realised then that this was perhaps Mick's Achilles heel. To put it quite bluntly, he needed cash so that he could 'cut a dash', especially with the ladies. I realised also that Mick's true identity, previously masked by the anonymity of prison life, was unquestionably that of Mick the Lad and it was unrealistic to hope that he would easily become Michael the Student.

That the academic ability was there, I had no doubt, but where there is no will, there is no way. It was fairly obvious where Mick's enthusiasm would lead him. As his stature as an assistant to Rose at the YMCA grew and his cash earnings with it, he spent more and more time at the YMCA and less and less time at Junction Road. As a result, he was not discharging his responsibilities to Georgie and his commitment to academic work began to fall apart. The question of the rent-free accommodation at Junction Road therefore became an issue, but Mick solved that problem in the manner one would expect of him. He pursued a relationship with a girlfriend who happened to own a residential property of which she was the sole occupant. Did Mick fall in love with the girl or with the property? We shall never know. The choice of girlfriend, too, was most unfortunate, because she herself had connections with the Junction Road hostel. Much distress and embarrassment arose when the relationship came to an end and it was alleged that Mick had run up considerable debts in her name. Of course, this sort of behaviour did nothing to strengthen relations generally, and certainly at the time I quite wrongly came to the conclusion that Mick's main concern seemed to be the recovery of his street 'cred' rather than the more lofty ambitions which we had envisaged. My error of judgement arose because I failed to realise that we were trying to do too much too soon. I had also underestimated Mick. He knew where his personal ambitions lay and he was, of course, free to pursue them. His personal life may have caused a few eyebrows to be raised, but one fact remained solid. He continued to discharge his duties at the YMCA to Rose's complete satisfaction, and he grew in stature and seniority by the day. He also earned good money in the process, and that remains the position to this day.

On reflection, therefore, much encouragement can be drawn from the outcome of what had been a particularly hard path to rehabilitation. Mick has a real job at last. It is a job to which he is totally committed, that interests him, that he is good at, that pays reasonably well and is there for the long term if so required. Mick is also off drugs and seems to have well and truly learned his lesson on that score. At the same time, I still think that with a few more years' experience at the YMCA under his belt, together with some ongoing preliminary academic study, Mick could be a candidate for a sociology diploma course that might in turn lead on to a degree course. That would enable Mick to move into a fairly senior position with the social services, while still concentrating on youth work with the disadvantaged. But that is not Mick's choice at the time of writing. Nevertheless, although I think we could fairly record a 2–1 victory in the case of Mick's rehabilitation, I would prefer to consider it a half-time score. Certainly, it has been nothing if not a valuable experience anyway.

Chapter Five

Political Correctness from the Home Office

'Practical politics consists in ignoring facts.'
Henry Brooks Adams (1907)

In early December 2001, I was approached by my good friend Simon Frith, who asked if I would be interested in serving as a volunteer member on one of the new youth-offending panels which were to be set up in the New Year. Simon, who headed up the local youth-offending team, was of course aware of my work at Junction Road. It was to Simon that I would turn for professional advice during some of my more hectic times there. Simon had been saddled with the responsibility of recruiting panel members for the new scheme. I was therefore halfway to an immediate 'yes' to his invitation as a measure of my personal support for him.

There was another factor that came into play and influenced my decision. A number of our residents had found themselves up before the youth or magistrates' courts during their time with us. They were not master criminals but slipped easily into and out of petty crime as a result of peer pressure. This skirmishing with the law and appearance before the magistrates was to some of them a fact of life and seemed in no way a disincentive towards further criminal activity. I was appalled at the contempt with which these young men viewed the law and all the apparatus that went with it, including the judicial system. I have heard young men still in their teens, actually boasting as to the quantum of their latest fine affixed by the magistrates. A fine of £300 carried with it more kudos than one for £100. And, of course, hardly ever would the fines actually be paid. A payment schedule would be arranged calling for what would be described as affordable payments to be made on a weekly basis. The payments would start at week one and fade out in about week four. That would start a paperchase of reminder letters and various threats, all of which would be ignored. One of our lads owed over £600 in unpaid fines. He was threatened with imprisonment unless he made a substantial payment on account, which was about as realistic as asking the young man to take up the next vacant place at the Hendon Police Training College. As a result, the young person disappeared into Glen Parva Young Offenders' Institution and reappeared one week later with his debt expunged. He was delighted. The cost to the taxpayer was in excess of £2,000. Such was the madness and ineffectiveness of the then system or lack of it. If joining Simon's recruits would provide an insight into how the proposed new methods might work to help restore respect for the judicial process, then there could be value in my participating.

The new arrangements were well covered by statute. The Youth Justice and Criminal Evidence Bill, which received its Royal Assent in 2000, provided for the mandatory referral of young first offenders to youth-offending panels, as first outlined in the final chapter of the government's 1997 White Paper, entitled No More Excuses. Under the new statute, referral orders to the new panels were to become the standard sentence imposed by the youth or magistrates' courts for first-time offenders under the age of 18. Where such an order was made, the courts were not empowered to impose any other sentence by way of community order, fine, reparation order, conditional discharge, the binding over of an offender or his or her parents or guardian, or a parenting order.

These new arrangements certainly marked a radical change to the approach under which the first-time youth offender was to be dealt with. Proceedings were to be taken out of the rigid and often oppressive atmosphere of the magistrates' and youth courts and put in an altogether more informal setting divorced from the usual legal trappings. The suggested panels were to comprise two volunteer lay members and one member from the local youth-offending team. Those called to attend the initial panel meeting would include, in addition to the three panel members and the young offender, the victim of the offence and, if deemed necessary, a member of the local victim-support group. Others ordered to attend might include a designated person to assist the young offender (usually a parent or guardian but not a solicitor) and any other person who might be helpful to the proceedings – perhaps a teacher, friend of the family, social worker or the like. One of the panel's two lay members would take the chair and encourage a free discussion as to the full circumstances of the offence and how the various interested parties now felt about it (particularly the young offender and the victim). Discussion would then be encouraged as to the factors which might have led the young person to offend and the sort of interventions (remedies) that could now be put in place to assist the young person in not reoffending. These interventions might include, for example, anger-control sessions, help with alcohol or drug addiction, contributions from other specialist agencies, a home curfew, change of school, change of friends/peer group, improved communication with parents/guardian and so on. There was then to be further discussion to decide what would be a proportionate punishment and/or fair restitution to the victim, having regard to the offence committed and the loss suffered. A car window smashed and items stolen from the vehicle might be linked to the cost of replacements paid for by running an early morning paper round. Racist slogans daubed on a shop window might be linked to the clearing of all graffiti from the public lavatories. Throwing missiles into the garden of an elderly lady might be linked to the weekly cutting of her lawn. These were the sort of 'punishment fitting the crime' measures that might apply. The end product of the initial panel was then to be expressed in the form of a written contract, in ordinary rather than legal language, signed by the young offender and the panel chairman. This was to set out clearly those measures which the young offender was to undertake by way of intervention together with the agreed items of proportionate punishment or restitution.

Supervision of the young offender's various tasks as set down in the contract was to be the responsibility of the youth-offending team acting through their representative, who had served on the relevant panel. Any breakdown in performance by the young offender would trigger a further meeting of the panel and a call for an explanation as to why the contract had been broken. Further failures or refusals could result in a panel resolution to refer the young offender back to court for resentencing. If, on the other hand, the young offender completed his contract satisfactorily, then a final panel meeting would be held at which the young offender would be formally discharged. Under these circumstances, the young offender's name would not be registered in criminal records. This was deemed to be a powerful incentive for a young person to pass through the new procedures without mishap.

It was thought that the sort of informal setting in which the panel meetings were to be held would also be conducive to obtaining positive results. Those attending the panel meetings would sit in easy chairs grouped around a round table that would be the central feature, replacing the magistrates' bench and the formal air that it tended to project. In addition, it was felt that the presence of the victim and the opportunity for the young offender to speak up for himself, rather than through a legal representative, would encourage a fuller and more open discussion as to what had happened, why it had happened, what might have prevented it happening and what could now be put in place to avoid it happening again. It was also hoped that such a discussion and, in particular, the confrontation between the young offender and his victim in such an 'informal' atmosphere might lead to gestures of regret from the young offender and might at least partly recompense the victim for the damage and injury caused.

Such was the extent of the new proposals. They certainly appeared to hang together well enough in terms of principle and intent, but how would they work out in practice?

Of course I was not privy to the proposed arrangements in detail when I attended the formal interview, which took place in early January 2002 at the offices of Northamptonshire Magistrates' Court. There I was certainly given a good general idea as to what was afoot, and I had one or two reservations.[1] But I swam along with the other successful applicants anxious to learn more.

There were perhaps 60 or 70 of us lined up to participate in the new experiment, and I first met my new colleagues when we all donned our name cards at the first training session. We had previously been given a choice of training sessions to suit our personal circumstances, and I plumped for the four all-day Saturday sittings,

---

[1] I had some inward disquiet as to the involvement of government, not the most welcome of bedfellows as far as I was concerned. Would we be bombarded by directives from the Home Office telling us what we should do and how we should do it? I was also concerned as to what effect the new responsibilities might have upon my work with the residents and ex-residents at the hostel. Finally, I was aware that we were dealing with an essentially practical subject. Its transfer from theory into practice would be the acid test.

risking complete brain seizure by about the sixth hour. The sessions took place in rather sumptuous offices situated in a fairly new development at Brooke House, just outside Northampton's eastern outskirts, which suggested that the new project was being well funded either by local or national government, or both. My fellow trainees were predominantly middle-class, middle-aged and female. I learned that a good number of them already had experience of working with young people in the National Health Service or social services in one capacity or another. A number of them were themselves mothers with teenage children of their own. There was therefore present in the audience before the lecturers got at us a good store of knowledge and experience as to teenagers and their problems. Perhaps if they weren't going to be taught how to suck eggs, then maybe as panel members they were going to be taught how to suck some rather special addled eggs. I counted only two volunteer trainees from ethnic-minority backgrounds among our total number of 60 or 70 – which was rather sad – but there was definitely at least one homosexual gentleman among our number. I know that was the case because for reasons best known to himself he kept reminding us of that fact at almost every training session.

As a bunch, I found my trainee colleagues friendly, cheerful and always ready for a laugh. But, they were also intelligent, articulate and, like me, curious as to where the training course would lead us. There is something very attractive about the British middle class when their noses are raised in anticipation and curiosity. Being British, everything must of course be kept firmly under control. Is there such a virtue as stoic enthusiasm? If so, it belongs to the British middle classes. But these people were middle-class with a difference. They were reaching over the garden fence to try and help those young people who had perhaps lost their way. They were middle-class plus.

The training sessions themselves were efficiently presented and professional in content. With Simon in charge, I would have expected no less. Lectures took up most of our time in the early sessions. They were interesting and practical, very much to the point, and linked up well with notes contained in our individual Home Office workbooks. The lectures were delivered by Simon and his colleagues from the young-offenders team, with one or two outsiders dealing with specialist subjects. All the lecturers were fieldworkers – that is to say, their knowledge came from what they did, not from what they read about. They engaged our interest and respect accordingly.

76

They emphasised the essentials and skipped around some of the Home Office detail, but above all they certainly made clear to us the relevance of their remarks to the ultimate purpose of the panels upon which we were to serve.

As to the actual content of the lectures, there was certainly enough to ensure that I was thoroughly brain-addled by the time I fell into my car on each successive Saturday evening. Of course, in the main we discussed modern teenagers. Metaphorically, we submitted them to a very personal, systematic and critical examination – stripping them down, dismantling them and then reassembling them in our attempts to identify the factors that make a 'normal' one tick and an 'abnormal' one explode into criminal activity. We were then introduced to the myriad interventions that were available from specialist sources, which might be able to counter at least some of the weaknesses thrown up by our analysis of the offending teenager's lifestyle. Drug-addiction advice, help with alcoholism, anger control, general counselling, advice with sexual-orientation problems, help with race relations and even psychiatric help were all examples of the sort of special services we could plug into as required. We also dealt with that part of the equation which was being brought into the centre of things for the very first time by the new legislation, namely the victim.

The confrontation between the victim and the young offender at the first panel meeting might provide some fireworks, and would call for diplomatic skills from the panel leader no matter what theoretical advantage might flow from their presence. The victim might also be represented by the local victim-support group, who might well strengthen the victim's representations and harden their views both as to the compensation properly due to them and the sort of punishment to be shouldered by the young offender. Again, there might be a need for diplomatic skills before agreement could be reached by all parties. In fact, this seemed to be the crux of the matter. There had been criminal activity. Half a dozen people may have been affected, either directly or indirectly, and it was probable that each would have a very different view about the incident and its consequences. To obtain at the end of the first panel meeting a contract signed by the young offender undertaking to make agreed reparation or compensation to the victim and to bind himself to undergo agreed intervention measures to assist him in overcoming his difficulties, and all this after all parties have had full opportunity to state their case, would, it seemed to me, require considerable management and diplomatic skills.

In the latter stages of our preparations we started to enact practice-run panel meetings given a particular set of circumstances surrounding a first-time offence by a young person.[2] We would split up into groups of seven or eight and then take it in turns to play the different characters attending the panel meeting, the interested parties as expressed in the example. Emphasis was always placed upon following the correct procedures – introductions, discussion (all contributing) as to the offence, the possible weaknesses in the offender's lifestyle, the interventions needed to help the offender, the reparations for the victim and the punishment of the offender, the agreement of the contract and its signature. As practice run followed practice run they became like little playlets, all following the set procedures and programme with the same sorts of characters, the same sort of offence and the same sort of conclusion. The Home Office workbook was full of such examples. It all seemed so neat and tidy and inevitable. Too much so, I thought. I hoped the real thing would be more than a playlet. Certainly, in retrospect I know it was at this point that I began to have my doubts about the real worth and purpose of what we were doing.

There were two matters in particular that had begun to worry me, because neither squared with my own experience. In the early days, Pip Bailey was subject to recurrent bouts of bad temper. As a result, he was sometimes involved in physical assault without apparent good cause. If he had come before one of our panels charged with physical assault, in accordance with our procedures he would almost certainly have been referred to the prescribed 'anger control' sessions as the appropriate intervention – and that would have got him and everyone else nowhere. The real cause of Pip's explosions of anger and their physical expression was his father's desertion of him, the disintegration of the family home and the arrival of a stranger as a stepfather. The suggested intervention would be treating an effect of the cause and not the cause itself. The true cause of Pip's well of anger was only brought to the surface through a relationship of trust built up over a matter of months, if not years. Pip would never have spilled the beans as to the real cause of his anger to a collection of strangers at

---

[2] Readers will appreciate that a young person categorised as a 'first-time' offender may have offended previously but has never been apprehended or charged. Some first-time offenders are not as innocent as they look or pretend to be.

a half-hour panel meeting or, for that matter, to another collection of strangers at any 'anger control' sessions. Pip was a very private young man and any calls for free and full discussion at a panel meeting would have fallen on deaf ears as far as he was concerned. He was not untypical either.

I was afraid to extrapolate. If I did I began to speculate as to the real purpose for which we were being trained up because the declared purpose didn't seem to hold up. The second point that worried me was that, although in many of the examples we worked through there were included characters of different ethnic and religious groupings, nowhere was there any suggestion by way of intervention that representatives of a young offender's religious faith should be involved. This seemed to me extraordinary. Many young men of (say) the Muslim faith would more readily share their innermost thoughts with their religious leader than with the strangers they would encounter on the panel. My discreet enquiries on this second issue led me, as I half-expected, to a brick wall. The new statute was the product of a secular government, and the Home Office workbooks from which we took our examples followed the secular theme to the letter. But the workbooks and the secular government were one thing and the world that I knew was something very different. Certain individuals – and not only those of Asian or other ethnic backgrounds – still held strong religious convictions which could be very relevant in a particular case. It seemed to me that in terms of common sense, if nothing else, it was a factor that could not be ignored. Unfortunately, it was ignored. I hoped that when reality eventually superseded our period of playlets, my fears would prove to be groundless.

In fact, my fears were only increased when as fledgling panel members we finished our training, received our certificates to that effect and took up our places on the real youth-offending panels. I was dismayed to find that the playlets format became the reality. None of the cases that I attended[3] lasted much more than half an hour. In accordance with our instructions, we followed the same strict procedures as in our practice runs, made the same sorts of suggestions as to interventions, reparations and punishment, and had everything boxed up and completed well within the hour. Our production run was such that we could easily have dealt with three

---

[3] Only three in total. I had seen and heard enough by then to know that I was fundamentally opposed to their method of operation. I therefore resigned my position

cases or more each morning. But what purpose there was in such skin-deep revels escaped me – that is, until I put on my political spectacles, whereupon everything began to take shape.

My original fears were being fully justified in actual cases. The so-called full discussion, with all parties participating, which was supposed to lead us to the weaknesses in the young offender's lifestyle and the cause of his offending behaviour, fed generously from the pot of facile assumptions. There simply was not the time, or the resources, or the research, or the personal history, or any usable personal relationships of value to get anywhere but nowhere in terms of fundamentals.

Quite naturally and understandably, there was invariably nil contribution from the young offender. He knew he was being questioned by members of the Establishment. Whether they sat around a table or behind a bench or wore wigs or did not wear wigs was of no great significance to him. He would, and did, say the sorts of things that he knew the Establishment wanted to hear – things like 'I'm sorry,' 'I don't know what made me do it,' 'I'd had too much to drink,' 'I've got such a temper' – and the interventions and reparations would be marked up accordingly. Any real spilling of the beans in terms of fundamental cause and effect was a non-starter and, in my opinion, would ever remain so in the playlet setting of the new panels. How I longed at each panel sitting to relinquish my seat as a panel member and take on the job of the young offender's mentor in the medium or even long term. Then and only then might one expect to produce meaningful historical data and worthwhile help for the youngster concerned, based upon the patient building up of a relationship of trust. There was no relationship of trust at panel meetings simply because there was no time to build one.

The other weakness that I had mentioned – the failure to bring anything tainted with religion into play – was brought home to me forcibly at the last panel meeting I attended and was the immediate cause of my letter of resignation that followed. The case concerned a young Irish lad who had had too much to drink on New Year's Eve. That had led to an altercation in a fish and chip shop culminating in our young friend dancing on top of the serving counter brandishing a knife and threatening all and sundry. Enter the police. Exit the young offender, followed by his subsequent appearance before our panel as a first offender.

The young man's father had vanished from the domestic scene

80

years ago. His mother had refused to attend the hearing, as did the victims who had originally claimed to have been threatened. One family member did attend in support of the young man, however, and that was his grandmother. After less than ten minutes informal discussion with the grandmother, I ascertained that she was a Roman Catholic, that her parish priest was Canon James Galvin, who was well known to me personally, that she practised her religion assiduously, that until two years previously her grandson had done likewise, and that in a fortnight's time she would be joining a pilgrimage to the Catholic shrine at Medjugorje in Yugoslavia. I also could not help but notice that there was a real bond of affection between grandmother and grandson. When I suggested that his behaviour had let his grandmother down, the young man wept and instinctively embraced her. A glimpse of reality here. How best to build on it? The way ahead seemed obvious. Why not suggest to the young man that he should escort his grandmother on her pilgrimage to Yugoslavia, and with her help use that occasion to try and rekindle his own religious faith and to have a quiet think about his recent behaviour and the way ahead. And in the meantime, I would have a quiet word with Canon Galvin to ensure regular visiting and attendance upon the young man on his return. But such a sensible course of action was out of the question. It flouted a cardinal rule. It brought religious beliefs into play, and that was a mortal sin for a secular state living its life by secular rules. A secular solution had to be imposed – and was. We were soon talking about anger-control classes and advice on alcoholism. And my letter of resignation was as good as in the post.

There arose also a third weakness in the operation of the panel meetings, which pointed the finger at the difference between theory and practice. In none of the three cases with which I was concerned did a victim appear, although they were always invited to attend. On reflection, that was thoroughly understandable. Most reasonable people seek to avoid uncomfortable, embarrassing, unnecessary and possibly unnerving confrontations with unknown third parties, which is precisely what a victim might expect by attending a panel meeting at which the offender would also be present. As a result, I never saw a victim or heard a victim's views. A political clue to this quirky insertion of intent is perhaps provided by the title of the government White Paper which was a prelude to the new statute: No More Excuses was, I believe, a declaration of government intent to push the pendulum of justice towards the victim of crime and therefore away from the perpetrator in response to what was then considered to be the weight of public opinion. Thus does politics make for statutes firmly embedded in wishful thinking. There were other absences, too, from the theoretical line-up. I never set eyes on the father of any young offender, which apparently was par for the course. To me, the absence of this key figure in every case was crucial, but it seemed to concern no one but myself.

By the end of the third panel meeting I knew that I had to resign, and I did so. I could see no point to the existence of the panels other than to serve the political ends of the secular government of the day. In particular, the panels provided the thoroughly facile spectacle of appearing to deal with first offenders quickly and efficiently, with the victims at the very centre of things. In addition, the influx of several thousand panel lay members nationwide relieved the youth and magistrates' courts of much of their routine work and court congestion. All commendable political objectives, I'm sure, but hardly likely to whet the appetite of someone more interested in the problem of homeless youngsters in general and those at Junction Road in particular. So ended my adventure with Home Office political correctness. By way of appendance and conclusion I attach a copy of my letter of resignation to my good friend Simon. The reader will note that I have expanded on the main thrust of the contents of my letter in the later chapters of this book.

AS/SC

14 June 2002

Mr Simon Frith
Youth Offending Team
53 Billing Road
Northampton
NN1 5DB

My dear Simon

This letter is very difficult for me to write. At our meeting on Monday last I told you that I wished to resign from my position as a member of the Young Offender Panels. After considerable pressure from yourself, I agreed to stay on for a couple of months or so until things had settled down. I now wish to revoke that decision and revert to my original wish to resign forthwith. I am mindful that by so doing I have gone back on my word to you and that causes me no little discomfort.

The reasons for my decision to resign have, I hope, already been made clear to you at our meeting during which little was said that attacked my main line of argument. I feel also on reflection, that what you had to say as to the secular nature of the services provided by the YOT organisation reinforces me in my decision. I have to say also that your strong and sustained appeal on personal grounds for continued help in launching the project while much appreciated, was not relevant to the removal of my objections which were levelled at what the Panels were expected to do, even when launched and operating successfully.

My main objection is that the Panels (and the Courts for that matter) are ignoring the fundamental reason why young people offend which in my opinion, is the almost complete collapse of responsible parenting in the families that spawn the offender. Having by-passed this fundamental factor the Panels are then expected to concentrate their efforts on the effects flowing from the fundamental cause and intervene with a myriad of intervention agencies which attempt to deal with the peripheries rather than the root cause. A young man of seventeen does not need the services of anger management agencies, decision making agencies, drug and alcohol abuse agencies or ethnic group agencies etc. etc. etc. if he is resident with his natural father who is his role model, constant companion and friend, adviser, protector and moral teacher. But intent upon chasing the effects rather than facing up to the causes, a whole agency industry has been built up and there is every prospect of it proliferating further. You tell me that victims are not appearing before the panels. Will there be a consequent boost to the number and influence of the Victim Support Agencies? In this manner, all concerned can be very busy and convince themselves that they are doing valuable work. In the meantime, the underlying cause, unattended and ignored, will continue to grind out young offenders at a faster rate than the Panels will ever hope to cope with.

All that I have said is based upon my personal experience. I have only served on three Panels so far but as you know, I have spent the best part of ten years as Chairman of the Friends of Valerie Hanson House where I helped out with the homeless youngsters at Junction Road. Natural fathers were an endangered species there and any contact was with stepfathers, the mother's 'new boyfriend' or the mother's 'new partner', none of whom showed the slightest interest in the young person's welfare. Unwanted and unloved, role models for those young people were non-existent and the void was, of course, quickly filled by peer pressure, hardly a worthy substitute. As you know, the young persons in question were always one step away from offending and sometimes not even that.

In the last Panel case that I attended, the lad in question had lost two role models. His natural father had deserted him and his grandfather had died on him. Robbed of his rightful entitlement, is it any wonder that the young man had an inner anger which came to the boil during adolescence and which manifested itself in drunken and aggressive behaviour. The remaining pillar of strength within the fragmented family was the lad's grandmother with whom he had a great deal of affection. She was sustained by an active and positive religious faith. In my view, the interventions to help this young man should have been built around the grandmother and her (and his, even if lapsed) religious faith. None of this was covered in the YOT report and the young man departed with a mundane contract with the usual package of community work and prescribed alcohol abuse and anger control sessions. No attempt was made to deal with the lad's inner anger which had prompted his misbehaviour nor could it be in the open forum of the Panel. That required in-depth counselling on a one-to-one basis and I could have referred him to a Corby priest and personal friend of mine who could, in my opinion, have best provided that service. And to have the lad well groomed and ready to start such counselling sessions, I would have had the lad accompanying (and looking after) his grandmother on her forthcoming pilgrimage to Yugoslavia and to Sunday Mass with her for a 4-week trial session.

I think I have said enough to illustrate how fundamentally opposed I am to the work of the Panels and indeed, even in some respect to the work of the YOT based as it is on secular considerations alone. I have to say that I deplore the secularisation of this country that I love so much. I firmly believe that the fundamental flaw to which I have referred – the collapse of responsible parenting – is a direct outcome of the sexual promiscuity which has followed in the wake of the liberal secularisation of the 1960s/1970s. I shall have to say as the secular state has sown, so it can now reap(!)

I shall continue to function as long as I am able. I have always favoured the mentor approach to the problems of young people because it lends itself to the long term relationship and role model function which attends the fundamental need. My aid, as has been the case over the last ten years, will be prayer rather than self perpetuating agencies.

Finally and importantly, I hope there is nothing that I have said that will disturb in any way our friendship which I hope will continue to blossom. You have always been a great help to me over the years and my own role model in terms of patience, perseverance and tolerance in dealing with young people. You must understand and continue to be an answer to at least one of my prayers.

Yours sincerely

(Smithy)

Chapter Six

Our Lovable Rogue

'Youth is a blunder, manhood a struggle.'
Benjamin Disraeli (1849)

If you live in one of those smart, suburban, detached houses on the south-western outskirts of Northampton in the fashionable district of West Hunsbury, you might have answered an early-morning knock at your door. On the doorstep would stand a young man politely enquiring if you needed your windows cleaned. A quick glance at the young man himself and, over his shoulder, at his smart little Ford van (duly licensed, taxed and insured) with ladders and buckets aboard would convince you that this was no cowboy outfit. The young man himself would also impress – a handsome chunk of late-teenage manhood, clean and well groomed, soft-spoken and respectful in both tone and demeanour – and, once you had inevitably taken him on, he would work with diligence and an attitude of wanting to please. He would then depart having enquired as to a possible future appointment and whether you might like to have the window sills cleaned and the guttering cleared out in the spring.

At the close of the day and having completed his round, hopefully adding a few more new customers to his carefully kept register, our young man would then return to his own home with his pockets filled with the rewards of his labour. His home is anything but grand – rented accommodation on a short lease (in a less salubrious district of Northampton than West Hunsbury), second-hand furniture in the main, self-decorated, with DIY adaptions and so on. That is because our young man has not long been living independently, having spent most of his earlier life in care hostels and foster homes. In seeking an independent life, very little help by way of cash or kind or encouragement has been possible from family sources.[1] And because of his earlier troubled life he has also been denied the benefits of a settled home life and a proper education, which might have led on to a worthwhile career with concomitant income.

He does however have one jewel in his crown, which helps sustain his efforts to overcome all these difficulties and make something of his life. There is a girlfriend, Sue, who is his loyal partner, constant companion, true friend and adviser and, not least, valued bed companion. To make up the numbers in our young man's household there are also various small children of mixed parentage, some of whom appear to be permanent fixtures and others who seem to appear and disappear at irregular intervals. Last but not least, there is a Labrador bitch which produces litters of puppies from time to time to add to the fun. In material terms our young man owns very little, but still he seems to possess a great deal. I think he realises that.

The name of our young man is Michael Joseph Daly. We used to call him our lovable rogue. But not now. He has grown up.

If you could represent all the dozens of young men who passed through our hands during the ten years that I was in attendance at Junction Road so as to include all their common virtues and vices in one individual, then that individual would be Michael Daly. By the time he came to us at the age of 16, he was already a skilled street operator, having opted out of mainstream living years before that. His early life read like the proverbial horror comic, and his later life was peppered with petty crime. He was a handsome young man, rather in the style of a young Pip, with the same crinkle-cut jet-black hair, swarthy complexion (he claimed Irish/gypsy extraction) seductive brown eyes and infectious grin. He was extremely popular with his peer group, which he seemed to lead, mostly in the wrong direction. He was popular with the ladies, too, and was a father

---

[1] The Friends were able to help with the furniture.

before I met him and before he had reached his 17th birthday. He did, however, have one overriding saving grace, which was as welcome as it was unusual. It marked him out as something rather different from his peers. Somewhere, somehow, he had acquired an innate politeness and respectful attitude in social intercourse, which suggested an unusual inner dignity.[2] This plus an unfailing sense of fun and good humour made sessions of reprimand with him embarrassingly difficult. He was, if you like, the Artful Dodger of our community, typical yet special, if that be possible.

I first met Michael at an 18th birthday party for one of the lads. The occasion was celebrated at a Chinese restaurant and Michael had joined us as a new resident on that very day. He sat next to me and we chatted. I was surprised at his politeness and good behaviour, particularly in view of the street reputation which had preceded him. This outer crust made a welcome difference to the usual aggressive macho performance I was used to and had half-expected. But the events of a few days later were what made me realise that Michael Daly was likely to become a rather special case as far as my personal efforts were concerned.

It was my practice to attend the Northampton Kitchen each Wednesday morning, where I would help with the provision and serving of tea and sandwiches. (Some of our customers said that I made the best tea in Northampton. Others thought differently.) On the Wednesday following my Saturday meeting with Michael I was surprised to see through the serving hatch that he was in the kitchen pushing a small child in a pushchair.[3] I went over to have a word with him and, as I did so, a lady sitting a few yards away called me over. It was Michael's mother and she asked me to sit down with her. She was clearly very ill, but she clasped my arm very tightly and, knowing that I was connected with the hostel, implored me to do everything I could to help Michael. She was clearly especially fond of him and desperately wanted him to make something of his life because, she said, 'there is so much good in him'. It was as though the fates had conspired against (or for) me that morning. I had only met Michael three days previously and here was a special and personal plea from his mother on his behalf. I could not but try my best to do as she wished, and I thus resolved to do so.

---

[2] I cannot recall a single instance when in my presence he used the foul language common among his peers. In a barrack-room environment this characteristic was most conspicuous.
[3] It was one of his young half-brothers.

I saw Michael one evening later that week and had words with him privately in his room at the hostel. I mentioned my conversation with his mother without going into too much detail and made it clear that I would always be available to help him get a job or alternatively to take up a course of vocational training. How simple that seemed to be in terms of sensible advice and a worthwhile objective and yet how difficult to the point of impossibility I knew it would be having regard to the special circumstances of Michael's background, his chequered career to date, his reported street reputation and my previous experience with other residents. Michael listened carefully and politely to everything that I had to say and said next to nothing himself. Par for the course. Inner suspicion, a holding back, a lack of trust, fear of intrusion, threats to existing lifestyle, fear of required new lifestyle. I could read these thoughts, doubts and fears passing through his young mind as I spoke. I had seen it all before and I had no illusions as to the size of the problem. I was not therefore surprised or unduly disheartened when my early efforts were conspicuously unsuccessful. Michael flatly refused to 'go back to school'. The old chestnut was raised of the humiliations that would await him in the classroom because of his lack of basic education, but I knew that in his case there were more factors that were still undeclared. There were certain things that 'kings of the street' did not do, and going back to school was one of them. Michael claimed that he could hardly read or write and was therefore unfit to take up any academic vocational course. This claim to near illiteracy was soon to be disproved, but the inflexible attitude remained.

As for paid employment, Michael was far too busy to go to work. Subsidised by social security benefits, he lived a very active social life which seemed to involve half of Northampton's youngsters, male and female. In that capacity, he was king of all that he surveyed and he was not likely to throw all that overboard to take up a job that would mean migrating from the top of the pile to the bottom. I did keep reminding him that his continuing lifestyle, which involved no work and no studying but an abundance of socialising, was being funded by me and the millions like me who were providing the taxes to finance the Department of Social Security that fed into his personal pocket through the Job Seekers Allowance. If he didn't soon start doing the job-seeking bit, then the allowance bit would assuredly stop. Michael's attitude was that he would believe that when it happened – and he was sharp enough to know that no 16-year-old would be put out on the street without means of support.[4] If the system was there, he seemed content to use it and abuse it. I knew that the problem of going to work was a big one. It was apparent from his family background that, for one reason or another, Michael had never lived in a household that had subjected itself to the routine and discipline of getting up and pursuing any sort of regular day-on-day employment or day-on-day school attendance. That routine habit, which should have been normal to a young lad of 16, was completely absent in the case of Michael. As time went on, I realised just how fundamental this difficulty was in psychological terms.[5]

In those early days with Michael, I also had difficulty with the personal relationship itself. I had no occasion to take him out for any driving lessons as an aid to building that relationship for the very good reason that there was very little that I could teach him about driving a car. He had been driving (illegitimately) for years. In any case, I did not feel that such an exercise would have led to the early spilling of beans as far as he was concerned. He was a very private individual under his social and good-humoured exterior. It was not that Michael openly rejected what he may have considered an undue interference into his personal life. Rather did he ignore my efforts, or pretended to do so. There were times when I made appointments to see him at the hostel about his job prospects and the like that he would absent himself without notice. Of course, that was in no way a new experience. It was endemic with all the lads. To keep an appointment, keep a promise, tell the truth – these were just not in their rule book. But in the case of Michael, I would have hoped for something better if any sort of relationship had been developing. When reprimanded, he would apologise in that gracious manner of his which he could slip on for the purpose. But I knew that all my efforts were playing second fiddle to a lifestyle that showed little sign of change. I needed help. I got it from a man who became not only one of my most valued advisers but also a very good friend over the years.

[4] As those who recommend the reintroduction of the death penalty should be asked personally to pull the lever, so those who recommend the suspension of benefits to a 16-year-old should be asked personally to deposit the youngster on the streets of Northampton, where the criminal classes would assuredly and quickly claim him. Redemption is the only really effective course of action even for the most recalcitrant of youngsters, however long it may take.

[5] The reader will learn that later on, when Michael was almost forcibly compressed into the discipline of daily employment, genuine physical sickness resulted.

Simon Frith, in his capacity as head of the local young-offenders' unit, already knew Michael well.[6] He was unashamedly fond of the lad. His assessment agreed with that of Michael's mother, that there was 'a lot of good in him'. I explained to Simon that I was having some difficulty in finding this goodness and I would be grateful if he advised me as to the best place to look for it. Simon's advice made me realise that in my enthusiasm I was forgetting first principles. Simon reminded me that I was seeking within a matter of a few weeks to overturn a lifestyle built up over 16 years. I needed to hasten much more slowly and rely upon patience and perseverance for a long-term result. No quick fix was possible but long-term redemption could well be the case. I left Simon feeling like the complete amateur trying to do the professional's job.

There then occurred an event which in the end changed everything. It established our relationship on a much better footing, which was an important factor in bringing about the required radical change in Michael's lifestyle. Believers would describe the event as divine intervention, while others would refer to a most fortunate combination of circumstances (although it didn't look that way at the time). The event in question occurred on 6 February 1999 at Northampton Crown Court when Michael was for the first time ever sent to prison – or, to be precise, a young offenders' institution.[7]

The offence committed, to which Michael pleaded guilty, was that of causing grievous bodily harm by the severe beating of another teenager in Abington Street, Northampton on a Saturday evening after a bout of drinking. The street CCTV camera had caught the incident and the tape was rerun as evidence for the benefit of the court. I sat at the rear of the court and was appalled at what the videotape had recorded. I could not believe my eyes as I watched Michael on camera first knock the other youngster to the ground and then kick him about the body and even about the head. I could hardly disagree with and am unlikely ever to forget the judge's closing remarks as he sentenced Michael to 18 months

---

[6] Michael was not exactly a master criminal, but his exploits had brought him into contact with Simon. Michael's misdemeanours comprised minor offences against property rather than the individual and related mainly to the driving of vehicles without proper insurance, licence and tax. There were also items of petty theft and receiving stolen goods.

[7] The term 'prison' was not deemed politically acceptable to an electorate who might be unduly sensitive about the incarceration of 16-year-olds. Presumably, they were deemed less sensitive when the incarceration took place in a 'young-offenders' institution'. So Michael was sent to Onley Young Offenders Institution near Rugby.

imprisonment: 'You are a seriously disturbed young man and I have no hesitation in sentencing you to the maximum term of imprisonment according to your age.'

My state of shock as I sat there arose not from the fact of imprisonment but rather from the fact of the offence itself, which could only be described as a most vicious assault. On later reflection I realised of course that first principles again applied and explained everything. As with so many of our young men and so with Michael, there was an inner anger born of past humiliations and deprivations, and it only needed a spark (in this case a skinful of beer and an argument within the peer group) to set off the explosion and release all the pent-up anger and aggression which made up Michael's particular baggage. It's just that in Michael's case his exterior shell of politeness and good humour was so attractive that one was led uncomplainingly away from thoughts of explosive baggage. Certainly, up to the point of watching the video evidence in court, I had thought that Michael had been involved in nothing more serious than some sort of Abington Street fracas within his own peer group and that he would receive the usual proverbial slap on the wrists by way of punishment. When his case hardened to a charge of grievous bodily harm and transferred to the Crown Court I began to wonder, and when I saw the video in Court, I was devastated.

Michael had attired himself in his only suit for his Crown Court appearance. It was jet-black and of traditional cut. He looked very smart, more like a solicitor's articled clerk than a prisoner in the dock. As he turned away after sentencing he put on a brave smile, but I was wondering just how he would cope with the judge's public pronouncement that he was 'a seriously disturbed young man'. It was hardly conducive to boosting his self-esteem, any more than the life that now lay ahead of him in a penal institution would be. It seemed that instead of going forwards we would now be going backwards (in fact, as it turned out fortunately the opposite was the case). I was not allowed to see Michael as he was taken down, as I was not a relative, and the next time I did see him was a few weeks later when I first visited him at Onley Young Offenders' Institution near Rugby in Warwickshire.

Much has been written about the effect that an initial term of imprisonment in a young-offenders' institution has on those unfortunate young men so incarcerated. At Onley, the apprentice prisoner comes into contact with a crude, insensitive, overdisciplined, spartan regime where the rights of the individual are necessarily squeezed and subordinated to the control of a vastly overflowing but confined community. Many of the indignities suffered by the individual arise through unavoidable overcrowding. A cell for the individual is invariably shared by two and sometimes even three youngsters and that includes sharing the open lavatory facilities as well as the space. For the same reason, youngsters are 'banged up' (locked in their cells) for far longer periods than officially prescribed, with the subsequent risk of psychological disorder. Recreational and educational facilities are also kept at a minimum, 'because most of the inmates are on short-stay sentences and will soon be moving out'. To those young men with already well-developed outer protective crusts, such an environment invites them to grow their shields heavier, thicker and bigger so as to face up to the prison regime in true macho fashion. People such as these are eventually released with extra baggage and anger and added resolve to take on the system. The spell in the young-offenders' institution has done much by way of an apprenticeship to launch them into a career of serious criminality.

Not so Michael. He stuck his toe in the water, took the temperature and decided that he didn't like it. Prison life was not for him. Even in his earliest days at Onley he resolved never to go to prison again, and thus it has been. Michael could rough it with the best of them – no one had it rougher than he had in earlier life – and he could more than take care of himself in the hurly-burly of a hostile environment (and introduce a bit of fun into the proceedings on the way), but the knowledge that prison life, with all the privations that it entailed, was the inevitable end product of a criminal life seemed to impact on his young mind. I am convinced that Michael's spell at Onley was a significant positive factor in helping towards his rehabilitation after release.

There was another factor which I am sure also played a part. With a single exception,[8] I was about the only person who did not desert Michael when he took up his new residence at Onley. I was amazed at how the myriad friends who had surrounded Michael when he was on the streets of Northampton were suddenly absent. They did not visit him or telephone him or write to him (although that last option may have been difficult in some cases). It was just

---

[8] Georgie Doe, the then Manager at the Hostel (and see Chapter Seven).

like the proverbial fairy story. When things get tough, some of those you count as trusted friends melt away while others who you hardly count as friends appear at your elbow.[9]

For my part, I was only too pleased to make the best possible use of Michael's availability to make it known to him that the lifeline was extended and would always be so, and that I was genuinely concerned as to his welfare whether inside prison or outside it. I think that the truth of that simple message at last began to implant itself in the mind of my young charge as the months of imprisonment passed. I wrote to him regularly every week, giving him all the news from the hostel. I visited him as often as I could (laboriously jumping all the bureaucratic hurdles that procedure entailed), I brought him small bits and pieces by way of gifts to keep him going (I remember a book on boxing being a favourite), I remembered his birthday and Christmas and I even ferried his little son Kevin, together with Kevin's mother, to and from Onley for a special visit.[10] I also acted as a courier in connection with Michael's stuttering and waning relationship with his then girlfriend, relaying messages to and fro and eventually arranging a visit from the girlfriend to sort out their difficulties.[11] On that occasion I deemed it politic to busy myself with the refreshment machine at one end of the visitors' area while Michael and girlfriend exchanged intimacies or blows (as the case may be) under the watchful eye of the prison guard at the other end of the same visitors' area. And if all these good deeds were looked on as some sort of investment of my time, then the investment started to pay off – slow to start, the trickle of communication soon developed into a full flood.

As an educational exercise, I encouraged Michael to reply to my letters. At first, he did so with little enthusiasm and much trepidation. He had, of course, long claimed that he could neither write nor spell. His own letters proved otherwise on both counts. His handwriting was far better than mine. His spelling was such that it could be brought up to speed quite quickly by some intensive coaching and informal reading. I was therefore both surprised and delighted when

---

[9] A 'fairy story' that I know to be true from my own personal experience.

[10] A visit which was somewhat marred, as I remember, by a leaking nappy and the consternation caused among the prison staff when the call went out for emergency padding. It was the sort of crisis for which they had not been trained (any more than I had).

[11] All to no avail. When Michael returned to the hostel he was free of all female attachments, not that this unusual state of affairs lasted for long.

94

Michael's responses to my letters started to arrive. And there was something more. Not only was the standard of handwriting and spelling higher than expected, but there were also underlying powers of expression struggling to get out. All this I communicated to Michael, which gave him much encouragement. In no time at all, I was sending Michael regular weekly 'homework', which included exercises in numeracy as well as English, and Michael was responding with something very closely approaching real enthusiasm. A university lecturer could not have been more pleased by the results he was getting from his undergraduates than those I was getting from my pupil at Onley prison. That was because I had found what I had half-expected to find – an intelligence sadly neglected and encrusted with idleness but still ready to blossom for want of some honest-to-goodness formal teaching, encouragement and sweat.

I remember one piece of homework in particular. I asked Michael to imagine that he was the contender for the heavyweight boxing championship of the world and about to fight that delicate young man, Mike Tyson, for the heavyweight crown at Madison Square Garden, New York. I asked for an essay describing the event, expecting perhaps half a sheet of foolscap. I got over three pages. I also got an apology from Michael saying that he had run out of time, not ideas. The ideas were there in profusion demonstrating to me, as if it needed demonstrating, an imagination, application and enthusiasm, all of which cried out to be harnessed to some formal training. In painting his picture with words (admittedly often misspelled), he had referred to the noise of the big occasion, the bunting, the national anthem, the crowds, his supporters and friends cheering him on, Mr Tyson himself and the knock-out blow that consigns him to oblivion and places the heavyweight crown on Michael's head! Having thus proved the truth of something that I had long suspected – Michael's potential for further education – was there a chance that the same truth had been revealed to Michael? More importantly, would he be prepared to do something about it on his release?

Alas, in spite of the most impassioned advocacy from my side of the fence, that proved not to be the case. I think that Michael was genuinely surprised and pleased to demonstrate his academic potential during the enforced stay at Onley, and his self-esteem and confidence benefited accordingly. But it was the street and his 18 years' experience of it that beckoned him on his release rather than

95

the classroom, which still held hidden demons for him. An important by-product, however, was the establishment of the sort of personal relationship with Michael that I had been seeking ever since I had first spoken to his mother.

And so, in due course, Michael's period of incarceration came to an end. Georgie and I made up a bedraggled and damp couple as we waited in the early-morning rain at the side door of the prison on the day of his release. As he emerged, cheerful as ever with his bin-bag of worldly possessions slung over his shoulder and wearing the suit I had last seen at the Crown Court, I held the umbrella while Georgie embraced him. She then held the umbrella while I shook his hand. I remember wondering at the time if any young men came out of that prison side gate in the drizzle with no one at all there to embrace them or shake their hand. They would think the world was indeed a lonely and alien place.

Back at the hostel, Georgie had made Michael's old room ready for him, complete with an impressive display of 'welcome home' signs and bottled beers to fuel the inevitable celebration that would mark Michael's homecoming. Georgie was in the language of her young charges a 'diamond'. Like us all, she had a particular soft spot for Michael, which he knew all about and had often abused by bending and even breaking some of the hostel house rules. His friendliness, good humour, sense of fun and infectious grin had served him well in the past but, soon after his return, alarm bells began to sound in the higher echelons of the St Matthew's hierarchy, and the bells were impervious to Michael's personal charm. As a result, he soon found himself confronted with two simple choices – he could remain in residence at the hostel providing he undertook immediate full-time employment or a full-time course of vocational training or further education; or if that was unacceptable, then he must leave the hostel. The ultimatum was hardly unfair. After all, the conditions of residency remained those originally imposed on the day that the hostel had opened. Michael had lived long enough on his wits and very little else, but he had now reached manhood and he should have been showing signs of growing up.

His ultimate decision was to leave the hostel, though not before innumerable meetings had been held with him involving Georgie, Simon Frith and myself, all good friends who wanted to help but who also knew that the only person who could really help Michael was Michael himself. I pushed hard, of course, for resumption of his academic education, quoting the experience gained through the Onley 'homework', but I was faced with two problems. Michael was now beyond the age where he could undertake full-time GCSE O-level instruction at government expense and, in any case, he still refused to go back to school for all the old reasons. The thought of him at the ripe old age of 18, which he now was, struggling in a class of 16-year-olds was anathema to him. He did say that he would be prepared to continue with a programme of academic study, providing that he could do so privately with me as his tutor and after a struggle we were able to clear such an arrangement with Social Security so that housing and other benefits could continue.

But in the end, Michael opted to leave. He made the point that having attained his majority he preferred to spread his wings and make his way independently. Although he appreciated all that had been done for him at the hostel, he felt that the hostel house rules, regulations and routines had become unduly irksome to him. As I discovered later, he had forgotten to mention the most potent factor influencing his decision, namely his new girlfriend. But there was rather more to it than that. The new girlfriend, some three years older than Michael, had a small son by a previous relationship.[12] By reason of that status, she and the child occupied rented accommodation at the expense of the Social Security and Housing Benefit offices. It seemed that Michael, ever nimble in these matters, was poised to complete the trio.[13]

Michael's launch into so-called independent life therefore started on a rather sordid basis. He was in fact a kept man funded by monies provided by the Social Security and Housing Benefit authorities for his new girlfriend and her small son. Michael's contribution to the domestic budget was spasmodic and minimal, comprising the monies arising from his rather nefarious dealing activities, which would not warrant too rigorous inspection of their legitimacy. But there were factors in the new arrangements that within the space of a few years were to transform Michael's lifestyle

---

[12] The father was serving a term in prison at the time.

[13] Such an arrangement was of course out of order unless notification was given to the Social Security benefit office. If Michael took up occupancy, he would be deemed to be in receipt of an income and a supporter of the girlfriend and child. The Social Security benefits to the girlfriend would be reassessed accordingly. In fact, as in so many of these cases, boyfriends cohabited and double incomes arose without restriction of Social Security benefits.

and nudge him gently but firmly towards legitimate mainstream living.

Again, the believer would stand back and stare in wonderment at the divine spark which can transform human endeavour from an honest and unremitting but unavailing slog into a sudden triumphant march to the summit of success, one previously only dreamt about. The unbeliever on the other hand would refer to the special arrangement of circumstances suddenly gelling together to produce the unexpected. I had that very special feeling when I saw Pip Bailey perched on top of a combine harvester. I was shortly going to get that same feeling when I was to see Michael Daly perched on top of a window-cleaning ladder.

The first and most important of these factors which were to lead him to the promised land was the new girlfriend, Sue. She was something very, very different from the sort of sex partner usually passed off as Michael's current girlfriend. She was certainly physically very attractive – as fair as Michael was dark, small in stature and features, bright-eyed, shapely (very) with plenty of personality, but she was also much more than that. She was a strong character with plenty of intelligence. She therefore spoke her mind and had plenty to say. When she did it was like being under machine-gun fire, so rapidly did she speak. A shouting match between the two of them was a truly magnificent spectacle, which I was privileged to witness on more than one occasion. She was indeed a formidable character. Perhaps most importantly of all (at least at far as I was concerned), she joined hands with me in the need for a redemptive programme of objectives for Michael. She was determined that Michael should relinquish his more nefarious street friends, cut himself away from the fringes of the criminal world and think seriously about getting a job.

Of course, this was music to my ears. I thought that such a programme would be so unwelcome to Michael that the new girlfriend would soon become another ex-girlfriend. But I was wrong. It did not. It stuck and in due course went from strength to strength. I realised that the reason for that was because Michael himself, in his new-found wisdom, wanted to do everything that Sue and I wanted for him. If ever there was a case of the spirit being strong and the flesh weak, Michael was it. He really was growing up. His Onley experience had opened his eyes in more ways than one and now he had a girlfriend who was preaching the same gospel that he had heard from me since the day when I had first met him. The fates were beginning to stack up against him, but how could he, with our help, convert what was little more than wishful thinking into reality? How in fact could he sustain a full-time job, given his background, personal history and lack of employment skills?[14] I knew there were going to be very big practical problems ahead, however much Michael honestly recognised the need for change.

Meanwhile, Michael settled into the love nest. The accommodation, a council flat, was certainly adequate enough to house him and Sue and her son, young Justin. The location of the flat was not ideal – in a tower block in the Spring Boroughs district of Northampton, an area notorious for the activities of drug dealers and other undesirables. But it was home to the young couple and Justin, and they made it as comfortable as possible by redecorating and bringing in bits and pieces of furniture. And as there were no house rules to inhibit the few sparks and explosions along the way (which in themselves were magnificent to behold), the relationship grew in stature and understanding by the day.

As with the great fraternity of young men with whom I was then dealing, Michael's chief love in this life, apart from his new-found domestic bliss with Sue, was the motor vehicle. If he had any occupational skills at all they would have to be centred around motor vehicles and everything to do with motor vehicles. Of course, he was a fully proficient driver – certainly better than I was – but his licence was so peppered with penalty points[15] that insurance costs were astronomical and (legitimate) driving virtually impossible. Nevertheless, the interest in motor vehicles was followed up.

My eldest son, now senior partner in my local family firm of chartered accountants, rolled out his list of one-man-garage clients

---

[14] To readers in Middle Engalnd it is perhaps difficult to appreciate why such a problem existed. There are always plenty of unskilled jobs available. Why not grab one and get on with it? That is not easy for a young man of 20 who has never had a job of any description in his life, has never attended school on any regular basis and whose basic educational standards are thereby low, has no occupational skills, and has never been subjected to the disciplines of a well-ordered and well-run home. The psychological problems that arise in these circumstances are considerable, and I witnessed them at first hand.

[15] Almost all of them were for driving without insurance cover in a vehicle improperly taxed and (usually) without an MOT certificate. These points only dropped off the licence after a five-year period, so even when the proverbial new leaf was being turned over (as Michael had now begun to do), the virtual prohibition on driving remained. It was not much of an encouragement to new-leaf turning.

who might be interested in taking on a young man by way of work experience leading on to a government-sponsored apprentice scheme. He came up with the name of Nick Panter, who had a fine local reputation as a skilled automobile engineer.[16] I called on Nick and carefully explained Michael's special circumstances. I was delighted when he confirmed that he was willing to give Michael a chance. It seemed an ideal opportunity to get Michael's foot firmly on the first step of the ladder of mainstream living. Michael himself was excited, Sue thankful. We all (including Nick) must have prayed in our different ways that things would work out. In fact, they did not and, in the end, the experiment was almost a complete disaster.[17] It brought home to us all the reality and size of the problem that Michael had to face.

At first, he did well. Because he had no usable transport and was in the midst of turning over his new leaf, I used to pick him up at the flat each morning and run him down to the garage (a matter of a mile or so). Sue was charged with the responsibility of getting him out of bed, which I understand had its moments, but by and large he emerged from the tower block at the appointed hour. After week one, Nick gave him a clean bill of health, saying that he had worked well with 'beautiful hands'. I must admit that I had never examined Michael's hands, manicured or otherwise, but not being an engineer I failed to appreciate that Nick was referring to the manner in which Michael used his hands while working with the tools and automobile components in the complex business of stripping down and reassembling engines. After week two things started to go wrong. After week three everything went wrong and Michael was asked to leave, an event which caused me some embarrassment, but more importantly caused Michael considerable distress.

On reflection, there were many reasons why Michael's introduction to full-time employment failed. Some could be put down to the fact that Nick Panter's business was a one-man band. Nick's daughter was gravely ill (and subsequently died) during the period in question and Nick was unavoidably absent on that account, sometimes leaving Michael without work or proper instructions. The resulting boredom,

---

[16] It transpired later, after I had met him, that I had worked in the same office as his father, some 60 years previously.

[17] The only good thing that came out of it was the relationship I personally established with Nick which enabled me to help him with his business and tax affairs.

and his inability to deal properly with customers calling and requiring technical advice, was frustrating. There were, of course, no work colleagues, and it was often a very lonely shift that Michael worked – a very different environment to that which he had experienced on the street. And then, of course, there was precious little money. Work experience was what it said it was. The real money would come after the skills had been acquired, and that was going to be a fairly long haul.[18] But the most important fact of all was that these long-term prospects were to be founded on a daily discipline which involved getting up and getting to work at a fixed time each and every day for what must have appeared to Michael an eternity.

He had, of course, never been asked to respond to any such call to discipline throughout his life. Whether by good or ill fortune, every day that he had lived he had fashioned to his own requirement free of all interference. He had then lived for that day alone. Tomorrow was a different day. Parents, family, foster parents, teachers, social workers and sundry do-gooders had all been ignored in this extraordinary exercise of will and enterprise. The end product, inevitably, was an individual – lovable as he was – who paid no allegiance to, and was unable to live within the confines of, any sort of discipline, either internal or external.[19]

This was precisely what was being asked of Michael now. Appropriate lectures were given, and accepted in good faith, as to the worth of long-term investment in a job that would eventually bring skills, earnings and a worthwhile career. I can only say that if ever a young man tried to run that race at our behest it was Michael, but it was all to no avail. The reliability in the mornings began to slip and then Michael started absenting himself completely on the grounds of 'illness'. Of course, I was contemptuous of such a claim and was thus duly astounded to find, when I looked into it, that the reported illness turned out to be genuine. In all the years that I had known Michael I had never known him to be ill.

---

[18] This of course was eminently fair but Michael had attained his majority by the time he went to work for Nick. It was yet another example of how advancing years had not been matched by advancing skills (and income) with resulting resentment and loss of self-esteem.
[19] This was the most fundamental factor which prevented young men of the so-called teenage subculture, and with whom I had become acquainted, from taking up full-time employment. Simple disciplines which should have been taken on board as part of early home culture and carried on through schooldays were not in place and never had been. The psychological shock to those young men of a full seven-hour and a five-day week in full-time employment was not to be imagined. It was very real.

It was not difficult to surmise that the 'upset stomach' and the 'inability to sleep' could be ascribed directly to Michael's worry about the job and his inability to cope with it.

Finally, Nick, almost submerged in his own personal worries, and after extending the most generous latitude to Michael's now constant unreliability, decided in his wisdom to pull the plug and bring the experiment to an end. It was particularly unfortunate that, on the day Nick informed Michael that his employment was at an end, Michael and Sue had that very morning stood toe to toe having one of their shouting matches, which in this case had concluded by Sue telling Michael to vacate her flat. The double blow that Michael received that morning devastated his fragile world. As we sat in my car outside Nick's works and he explained what had happened that day, he wept in silent distress. I felt then as I had felt so many times before that the world could be so desperately lonely and cruel to those youngsters I now knew so well, who through no fault of their own lacked roots and family support to help them through life's difficulties. As Michael then explained, yesterday he had been living in a love nest with a girl he felt he really loved in spite of all the ups and downs, and he was trying his best to hold down the only real job he had ever had in his life. Today, he had nothing. No wonder he wept.

Fortunately, I was able to help him with at least half of his troubles. I had long since formed the impression that however many stand-up rows Michael and Sue might have, there was a depth of relationship which had developed way beyond the casual affairs that had littered Michael's life previously. Certainly, Michael's remarks in the car seemed to confirm that. Sue was a bit of a hothead (it went with her rather beautiful auburn hair). She didn't hold back when she had something to say, which was most of the time. Michael had been a leader on the street for years. He was unlikely to enjoy playing second fiddle to anything or anyone. Domestic explosions were therefore inevitable until such time as wisdom overtook the high jinks. As to the underlying relationship, I believed this to be strong. I therefore led Michael back to the love nest, made appropriate sounds and suggestions and then quietly withdrew. Later that day I was glad to hear that the lovebirds had resettled in their nest and relations were fully restored. Meanwhile, the other half of Michael's problem, his employment prospects, or lack of them, remained.

And so life went on. In the meantime Michael was able to get some casual-driving employment through agencies taking advantage of fleet-insurance policies. He also continued his dealing activities on the street and picked up casual-labour work wherever and whenever he could. Before the year was out, the young couple were able to move out of the unenviable Spring Boroughs district of Northampton and take up private rented accommodation in Abington, a much more desirable district of the town. During this time their relationship continued to strengthen. There were fewer and fewer toe-to-toe confrontations, and I could not but notice how easily and comfortably they conversed together, laughed together and enjoyed each other's company. An air of normality and permanence was beginning to descend upon them.

There then entered on the scene a character who became directly linked to Michael's salvation. He was an unlikely individual to play the part, but life is nothing if not an inveterate juggler of us all. The young man in question was a more recent resident at the hostel, being younger than Michael. Diminutive in size, bright-eyed and full of personality, he was aged 16 and looked 12. His name was John Higgins but he was called Chuck. No one seemed to know why. He claimed to have been driving motor vehicles for four years before he got to us. If so, it must have been a record. It had necessitated the use of a cushion on the driver's seat to enable him to look over the dashboard. He was the hostel's comic character. Not so to the Daventry constabulary. To them he was a 'pain in the arse'.[20]

Chuck came to us from Daventry under a care order, which suggests that there was a troubled and perhaps violent background to the case. Apparently, there was a need for a new start away from Daventry because of the bad company he had been keeping there. So he was brought to us at Northampton, where he was forever 'borrowing' motor vehicles from the streets and returning to Daventry. Once there he was inevitably picked up by the police and returned to us at Northampton. It was no joke but it certainly was a merry-go-round. It was reported that on one occasion, when summoned to appear before the magistrates' court at Daventry for driving a stolen car without proper insurance, Chuck drove there

---

[20] As officially described to me by the sergeant at Daventry to whom I spoke on more than one occasion.

in another stolen car without proper insurance, parked the car outside the courts on double yellow lines and then appeared before the magistrates and pleaded 'not guilty'. 'Pain in the arse' was a serious understatement of the position.

There were two distinguishing features to Chuck's character. He certainly showed us the extremes of a characteristic common to so many of our residents. In many cases, the line between right and wrong, legal and illegal, legitimate and illegitimate becomes somewhat blurred when temptation beckons. In Chuck's case, the line just never existed. If Chuck saw a car in the street that he fancied and felt that he would like to drive it, then he would take it and drive it.[21] The only principle that governed Chuck's behaviour was his own personal requirements at the time. His other, more positive distinguishing characteristic was that he worked. We had more than our fair share of young men whose bed was a much more beguiling option than their workbench. Not so, Chuck. From day one at the hostel (that is, when he was in residence and not halfway to Daventry), Chuck would jump out of bed and seek work – and, having found it, he would apply himself to it irrespective of what it was. As a result, Chuck was always earning money and spending it, sometimes to the unwarranted irritation of some of the lazier residents. I used to dream that if Chuck's plus points – his intelligence, personality and work rate – could be aggregated, then real progress for this young man might be possible, providing we could reinforce these qualities by introducing some semblance of discipline and by bringing his appalling behaviour under control. Alas, it was almost a lost cause. I had more than one session with Chuck to try and inject some sense of his own future into his thoughts, but I made little progress. Chuck was married to the street and he was interested in little else.

Eventually, his misbehaviour and, in particular, his cheek and lack of respect, which he seemed to reserve especially for the St Matthew's staff, brought about his inevitable exit from the hostel (and, yes, an inevitable return to Daventry). I was sad to see him go because there was so much in him that could have paid off given a little more patience and a lot more personal supervision and guidance. Needless to say that when he left, he had the last word. He had taken a dislike to a particular relief manager who

---

[21] Breaking into the car and turning the engine over was child's play to a young man of Chuck's experience.

104

had been in attendance during Chuck's last weekend. The manager owned a rather expensive Mercedes motor vehicle. Chuck's last act on leaving was to insert a suitably sized potato into the Mercedes exhaust pipe.

After his expulsion from the hostel it was inevitable that, having returned once more to Daventry, Chuck would again be shunted back to Northampton and that being Chuck, he would find work there. He was and did. It was also inevitable that being on the street in Northampton Chuck would sooner or later meet up with Michael, a respected elder of that fraternity. So when Chuck started cleaning windows for a previous employer who was looking for additional recruits in Northampton, what could again be more inevitable than that Chuck should approach Michael and ask if he would be interested in joining him. The remuneration to each assistant was based upon a set percentage of the gross 'take' arising from the windows cleaned by the assistant. The more windows cleaned, the more the earnings – and there were plenty of windows to go at, district after district.

After spending a few days balanced precariously on the top end of an extension ladder (during which he assured those concerned for his safety that 'all was well' even though he had an uncomfortable feeling that perhaps all might not be as well as he described),[22] Michael came to the conclusion that the prospect of his potential earnings was greater than his fear of heights. He therefore told Chuck that he was up for it. Of course, there was a technique to window cleaning and the public relations exercise that went with it, but these skills could be acquired with application and the gaining of experience. In any case, Michael was already a past master of the art of public relations. And for the first time, he could see how earnings could be linked with effort without the need for long periods of apprenticeship to learn the requisite skills. He was soon going home with substantial monies in his pocket, and he told me that he went to bed trying to calculate how many windows there were in Northampton that needed cleaning.

---

[22] I am reminded of the famous quote by Charles Dickens's Mr Pickwick. Mr Pickwick, more than a little inebriated, hauls himself to the roof of the stagecoach (there being no room inside). 'Is everything all right up there, Mr Pickwick?' shouts the coach driver. 'Yes,' shouts Mr Pickwick, 'all is well up here,' and Mr Pickwick has an inward presentiment that all was *not* well up there. But then Michael at the top of the ladder was presumably not drunk like Mr Pickwick on top of the stagecoach.

The next step, which was not long delayed, took both Chuck and Michael along the road marked out clearly in accordance with the tenets of the private-enterprise culture. Both of these young men correctly argued that if they had their own business and worked for themselves instead of other people, then the percentage of gross 'take' available to them after payment of expenses could be much increased. Furthermore, they could anticipate a position, providing the work could be obtained and they were confident that it could, where they could employ other young men as their assistants, providing they were properly instructed and controlled. All this seemed to add up at least in theory to good commercial sense, and so, again with very little delay, J & M Window Cleaning Services (proprietors John Higgins and Michael Daly) was duly born and made its bold entry among the ranks of those flying the flag of private enterprise.

Alas, our young enthusiasts had yet to learn that the progress of the successful entrepreneur is not one long uninterrupted march to the top of the sunlit plateau where the treasure chests lie, but rather a slow and tortuous progress based upon the principle of two steps forward and one step backward. In the case of our two young hopefuls, the first one step backwards was sufficient to blow all the fuses, bring the partnership to an end and send Chuck once again packing for Daventry, this time on a permanent basis. Of course, having regard to Chuck's record of irresponsible behaviour at the hostel – and, according to the relevant notes, for years before that – it would not be long before one could expect further instalments of Chuck's high jinks. They were not long in coming.

The most valuable asset owned by the partnership was a small Fiat Panda motor vehicle fitted out to carry the window-cleaning extension ladder and other equipment. The vehicle was permanently parked outside Michael's residence. On a particular weekend, Chuck took the vehicle to Daventry without permission and with the help of his Daventry colleagues used it and abused it as a private run-around vehicle and somehow managed to get all four tyres slashed in the process. All this, when he should have been in Northampton cleaning windows with his partner. It was like Chuck of old. His thinking never seemed to get beyond his immediate need – in this case, a vehicle that he could boast was his own, in which he could show off in front of his colleagues, 'joy riding' to his heart's content. The words 'obligation', 'duty', 'responsibility' and 'good faith' were never in Chuck's lexicon, and it was impossible under those conditions to build any sort of real partnership. So, with difficulty, Michael recovered the vehicle and rid himself of Chuck. Throughout the resulting trauma, I noticed that Michael never wavered in his ideas for the future, and in particular the opportunities that could arise if the window-cleaning project made progress.

This was, of course, evidence of his emerging maturity. All his recent experiences were bearing down on him and beginning to bear fruit. When he hit the buffers with his short spell in prison, it had brought home to Michael the reality of where street life would lead him. He knew also from that experience that help was and always would be available to him in his efforts to turn away from the street. Even the so-called failure of the Nick Panter experiment highlighted the fact that Michael had made the important decision to 'give it a go' and at least find out what mainstream living was all about. Never mind about what happened. The important thing was that the intention was there. It was for these reasons that the opportunity afforded by the window-cleaning venture was seen and appreciated for what it was – an entry into the real world of legitimacy, with earnings that would not depend upon a prolonged period of low-paid apprenticeship. But beyond these initial thoughts there were other, more extravagant ambitions. These ambitions grew with each day and were encouraged by Sue.

Michael wished rightfully to claim the role of breadwinner and respected father figure in a true family environment. That was what he wanted more than anything else. He had never known what it was to be loved as a small child, to live and be nurtured in a safe and loving environment, and he now wished to provide that sort of haven for those children for whom both Sue and he now felt a strong personal responsibility. In that pursuit, Sue stood four-square with him and was proud to do so. The roll-call of these children to whom Michael and Sue wished to extend their proposed protective umbrella was not short. Some were undoubtedly conceived at moments of sexual indiscretion, but their claims on responsible and loving parents were in no way diminished on that score. Rather were their claims enhanced.

Only one of the children they had in mind to make up their extended family was resident with them when Michael first took up his window-cleaning activities. This was young

Justin, aged three, Sue's son by a previous relationship. But Sue was also carrying Michael's child, and duly produced young John in the summer of 2003. Then there was Kevin, aged three, Michael's son by a previous relationship. Kevin was resident with his mother (Michael saw him at weekends), but Michael would dearly have loved to have him included in the plans for the future. The same applied to Michael's two half-brother twins, both of whom were in care and approaching their teens. No one knew better than Michael that such an environment had little to commend it in terms of keeping them off the street and away from criminal activity.

Of course, these domestic plans of Michael and Sue were ultra-ambitious, but how could one avoid giving them all the help that one could on their way? We live in a secular world where the collapse of responsible parenting is endemic in a modern-day culture which appears to list among its many extended freedoms the freedom to avoid personal responsibility for one's sexual behaviour. Here were two young people anxious to buck the trend and take on the supreme responsibility of caring for and nurturing the lives of those created through their own sexual union. Their courage in so doing is remarkable, their discerning morality humbling, their material resources few, their love for each other now profound. Not for the first time, I found myself asking the rhetorical question, 'Am I at this place to teach or to learn?'

I visited Michael and Sue's extended family (they call it their circus) just before last Christmas to drop off some seasonal presents. All five children were in attendance and a family dog had been added to make up the numbers. I even thought that I had been included myself as a further extension to the family when young Justin, noting the Christmas goodies, surprised me with his request when he greeted me with, 'Grandpa Smithy, will you bring me an Easter egg at Easter?' I felt that I had come a long way since my first meeting with the original residents at the hostel nearly ten years previously.

Rose Stewart ('Rose') on left and Georgina Doe ('Georgie') with the author at a Christmas party.

Georgie. She came as a cook and stayed as a diamond.

Lynne Rogers currently 'battling bravely on' as House Manager at Junction Road.

'It's really very simple, Smithy'. A veteran of the 'street' explains to the author.

We always made birthdays big occasions.

...and of course, Christmases too.

Our barbecues were very good at producing smoke.

The three wise men. One of them turned in 'A' grades at 'A' level.

Chapter Seven

Help from Above: St Matthew's Housing Society[1]

'You know very well that love is above all, the gift of oneself.'
                                   Jean Anouilh (1949)

My early days at Junction Road did nothing to shake my belief that very little in this world can be accomplished through the medium of a committee. As soon as the idea of the Friends was broached as a means of oiling the wheels of operation at Junction Road, a new piece of modern bureaucratic jargon was dumped in my lap. According to those with bureaucratic ambitions at St Matthew's Housing, the only way in which St Matthew's and the Friends could work in parallel and in harmony would be through the use of 'interlocking reciprocal committees'; that is, the Friends were to be represented on the local St Matthew's general committee and St Matthew's represented on the Friends committee. The very thought terrified me. I hardly thought that the principle of interlocking reciprocity would be of absorbing interest to the young men I intended to serve but, in any case, I had two good practical reasons for my distaste and opposition to the suggested linkage of interests.

In the first place, the Friends did not have, and indeed have never had, a formal committee to direct its affairs. From day one, its financial administration had been placed in the hands of an able

---

[1] In more recent times, abbreviated to SMH.

and very pleasant female senior assistant at my family firm of chartered accountants. Not only was she a first-class administrator, churning out regular financial and statistical reports as required, she was also very interested in the work we were doing, or trying to do, with the lads themselves. She was a pleasure to have around. In addition, from time to time I enlisted support and help from individual Friends and other local colleagues as the occasion demanded (particularly, for example, in the matter of transport). I was also joined from time to time by helpers on a longer-term, though somehow never permanent basis. My own commitment, however, soon became almost total, absorbing more and more of my personal time as my interest and enthusiasm grew with the years. Taken together, we made up an effective operational group, always available, quick into action, flexible, totally committed, and with increasing practical skills allied directly to the residents' well-being. But we had no need for a formal committee to confuse talk with work, to bog down and restrain our endeavours and drown us in paper. For this reason alone, the interlocking reciprocal enthusiasts were therefore never in with a chance. There was nothing with which they could interlock.

There was, in addition, a second reason for my wish to avoid the proposed mix of duties and responsibilities that I knew would arise through interrepresentation. My personal interest (and that of individual Friends who were making cash contributions) lay exclusively with the practical welfare and rehabilitation of the homeless youngsters who were going to be taken into care. I was not interested in the administrative functions at the hostel which underpinned this work – in the budgetary control of the hostel's finances, the difficulties with the Housing Benefit agency or the social services, or with rent arrears from residents, and so on. In view of my own professional background, I feared that if I sat on the local St Matthew's general committee I would almost certainly become entangled in such matters. No one would dispute their importance, but my interest lay elsewhere. My resistance to joint representation in those early days was therefore solid and total. It was only after the disagreement had spiralled upwards through the higher echelons of the St Matthew's hierarchy that it was finally resolved.

The occasion was a personal visit to Junction Road by the chairman of St Matthew's Housing Society himself and the 'full

110

and frank discussion' that followed. We then both had the opportunity of (quite vigorously) exchanging views. The St Matthew's concern was understandable. They were ultimately responsible for the well-being and safety of the youngsters in their charge, and for full compliance with all the statutory regulations that applied to the youngsters, who were of course, for the most part, juveniles. Where was the demonstrative accountability if the Friends were allowed to play fast and loose with their young charges without proper liaison and a chain of control leading back to St Matthew's? All of this was, of course, perfectly true, and made good sense. I therefore made it clear that I would take personal responsibility for ensuring that all the Friends' activities would be conducted only with the prior knowledge, agreement and cooperation of the local hostel management. They would then be able to report on the Friends' activities to the local general committee of St Matthew's as part of their normal reporting procedures. My personal assurance was accepted and we were able to proceed accordingly. Interlocking reciprocals were thus buried before they were born.

Our informal arrangement lasted for the full period of near ten years while I was in the saddle and, subject to one or two blips, was conspicuously successful. To say I was blessed with enthusiastic support from the hostel management is to understate the case. Not only did we gain their support, we also embraced ideas and suggestions emanating from them and even from the residents themselves. The degree of cooperation we received varied to some extent according to each individual hostel manager. Some gave unstinting cooperation. Others gave perhaps less. But, generally, our relationship with the St Matthew's Society flourished and that included not only with our local contact in Northampton, but also with their district office at Peterborough and head office in Norwich.

In my dealings with St Matthew's, I was always mindful that, when they were first approached by Valerie Hanson to open a hostel for homeless youngsters between the ages of 16 and 18, the project represented a leap in the dark as far as St Matthew's were concerned. They had established a well-deserved reputation for the provision of accommodation for the homeless and disadvantaged throughout East Anglia, but had never provided a self-contained hostel to cater exclusively for homeless young men who might qualify under the general description of 'young tearaways'. It took courage and a true vocational outlook to give the go-ahead to Valerie. But they did so, and I know that as a result scores of youngsters here in Northampton were taken in, looked after, cared for and shown how they could lead a different and better way of life. Not all of them took up the option, of course, but a good number did, and I am sure that in later years the youngsters will reflect on that, as indeed St Matthew's should, with considerable pride.

Towards the end of my own near ten-year tenure at Junction Road, St Matthew's made the decision to dilute the mix of residents by introducing older individuals, both male and female. They felt that a more mature entry would have a calming effect upon life generally at the hostel and lead to a quieter, more tranquil and less troublesome atmosphere. I believe that has been the case. I also believe that St Matthew's probably found that a mix of residents was easier on the cost budget than the original basis, which almost certainly involved higher labour and other costs.[2] But this decision was a matter of policy for St Matthew's and they alone were aware of the facts that determined the policy. For my part, I was unhappy with the 'watering down' of the intake of young men, because that was the hostel's original purpose; and my experience told me that the need for such accommodation and, as importantly, the influence that went with a hostel place, was greater not less at the end of my ten-year stint. I was not therefore unhappy that my own retirement from duty should coincide with St Matthew's change of policy.

But for almost all of my ten years original policies prevailed and, together with the hostel manager *in situ*, we went busily along doing what we could to bring some measure of hope and self-esteem to young men who had all but lost those qualities. As already indicated, the degree of support the Friends received from the hostel management depended very much on the particular individual in the saddle. I can recall two hostel managers – one male, one female – where the cooperation was minimal. It needed only two or three weeks' experience of working with them to know that both viewed their appointments as not much more than a stopgap means of acquiring living accommodation and an income. Their interest in the well-being of the residents was minimal. It was matched by their interest, or lack of it, in the activities of the Friends. Fortunately, neither survived more than a few months.

---

[2] With a 'full house' of youngsters, a full-time assistant to the hostel manager was essential. With a mixture of residents this post became unnecessary and was abandoned.

There were also various assistants appointed to the hostel staff who served for varying periods and showed varying interest in the Friends' activities.

One was an Oxford graduate who had studied psychology. He described his time at Junction Road as 'valuable practical experience'. He also conceded when leaving that he was punch-drunk. Nevertheless, he was a great favourite with the lads and contributed much to the Friends. We were all much saddened when he left. Another university graduate joined Chris Atherly as an assistant in the early days. St Matthew's informed me when appointing him that he was anxious to try his vocation in 'handling difficult young men'. He departed after only a few months. I think he had convinced himself that whoever might have a vocation in handling difficult young men, it was not him. But all this and these were mere peripherals to the larger picture at Junction Road, which reflected a vast amount of good work originating from an enlightened hostel management and the enthusiastic cooperation of the Friends. That good work centred around the efforts of three particular hostel managers who served during my time. Significantly, all three were female.

Rose Stewart, Georgina Doe and Lynne Rogers all served for fairly long periods,[3] which enabled them to establish their personal reputations and to build up the essential relationship of trust with their young charges. Taken together, these three hostel managers served in that capacity for the vast majority of the time I was active with the Friends. I was therefore able to observe at close quarters how each one of them tackled their responsibilities in quite different ways. But there was one factor which was common to all three. It marked them down as individuals of particular calibre and in my mind bound them all together. If love is indeed 'above all the gift of oneself', then the love of these three individuals for the youngsters in their care was demonstrated to me over and over again through the years. It was a humbling experience. We live in a very selfish material world. Life at Junction Road was anchored in something very different. I was again befuddled by the question, 'Am I here to teach or to learn?'

Rose Stewart reminded me very much of my own mother. She was small, wiry and tough, with a dominant personality and an

---

[3] Lynne is still in the saddle at the time of writing.

inexhaustible fund of energy. And as I was later to discover, she was fuelled by a very strong personal credo. That made her a very formidable individual. She followed Chris Atherly as hostel manager and served in that capacity for several years. In my opinion she was the major catch by St Matthew's that guaranteed the future success of the Junction Road hostel. In only one respect was she different from my mother. She had sad eyes. Maybe they were saddened by her own troubled personal history. It was not until months into our relationship that I became aware of this history. Rose knew all about the rough end of both physical and mental abuse and all about the indignities and humiliations that went with that state of affairs. I later realised that these experiences from her past were one of the sources of the extraordinary compassion and understanding which she showed constantly in her dealings with the young men in her care. It was almost as if she were saying, 'I know how you have suffered. I have been there myself and I am here to comfort you.' If Chris Atherly knew how to establish a relationship with a young man, then Rose Stewart knew how to reach that young man's heart.

There was also another reason for Rose's rather special approach to life and those around her. She quite freely advanced the reason herself but claimed no personal credit. Again arising out of her past experiences, she had become a born-again Christian. She practised her religion assiduously, and it became increasingly clear that her lifestyle was dictated exclusively by the tenets of her faith. She never pressed her views on anyone else and certainly not on any of the residents. If she was looking for converts I remember thinking that they would come from her example rather than any argument she might put forward. She did explain to me on one occasion that, as far as she was concerned, 'Thy Will be done' meant the work at the hostel and the needs of the residents. She reckoned that task was her personal calling, an obligation to her Maker irrespective of her own personal wants and desires. To her there was an intellectual decision underlying her emotional involvement, and it was as simple as that. Maybe things are as simple as that to one cloaked in Rose's philosophical and religious beliefs. Certainly, her demeanour over the years was such that it seemed to me she was either someone prompted by a genuine divine spark or, alternatively, she was just a very remarkable woman. Perhaps a combination of both. I just counted my blessings that I

114

had such an experienced and competent colleague to work with and from whom I could learn much. She made that easy too. There was no strident assertion attaching to her wisdom.

And so it proved. It was Rose who formalised the first advice that I had ever received at Chris Atherly's elbow: no communication without relationship; no relationship without trust; no trust without patience. Rose made it known to her young charges that she trusted them at all times and in all circumstances. She might first speak to a lad, or all of them, and lay everything on the line so that they were clear where the lines were drawn: 'You will be going into town on Saturday evening. I expect you to have a drink but I trust you not to have too much to drink.' If things went wrong, there would be reprimand and punishment if necessary, but Rose would continue to extend her trust to the young man concerned. Eventually, the penny would drop and, in many cases for the first time in his young life, the youngster would realise that Rose was not only a person he could trust, but perhaps even more importantly one who was prepared to trust him. That realisation gave a tremendous boost to the dignity and self-esteem of the young man and led in certain cases to a strong bond of loyalty which affected us as well as our young men.

I remember Rose warning me that we had to be careful that this bond of loyalty did not blind us to the facts of life. The progress of our young men towards mainstream living usually took the form of two steps forward and one step backwards. Unfortunately, the single backward step sometimes attracted the attention of the local constabulary. Unlike us, they were unaware of, and in any case had little interest in, the two steps forward. It was the one step backwards that excited their attention, which to us ignored the bigger picture. Our lads were not master criminals (we had no armed robbers on our books) and our loyalty to the lads tended to promote an anti-police attitude. Rose knew this, foresaw the danger and stamped on it. As a result, relations with the police remained friendly and cooperative at all times,[4] even though our young men continued their indiscretions.

---

[4] The best (and most ironic) example of cooperation with the police occurred when there was a daylight street mugging and robbery in Junction Road. A police squad car arrived and invited our 'lovable rogue' (see Chapter Six) to join them in the squad car as they toured the district so he could help identify any doubtful characters who may have been responsible. It is the only occasion when one of our lads was appointed to the position of special constable.

It was also Rose who instructed me in the delicate art of reprimanding our young men for their transgressions as and when the occasion arose. She placed special importance on the exercise. It was unfortunately the case that a good number of our young men had experienced countless reprimands in one form or another (which in some cases could be more accurately described as mental abuse) from the day they were born. One would therefore have thought them impervious to any new round of the same thing, particularly if the armour-plated macho behaviour which had served them so well in the past was still in place. But, as Rose pointed out, we hoped that the armour plating had slipped a little as a result of our efforts to create a new climate of trust. If that were the case, we were dealing with something very different – a fragile young man who we hoped was about to come out of his shell. The important difference now was that the reprimand was coming from someone the lad might respect and trust. It needed therefore to be administered very carefully so that the respect and trust was maintained.

Rose always recommended what she called the 'sandwich' approach. She used to tell us to lead off with a statement of the lad's attributes and how pleased we were with his general progress, then explain carefully why the reprimand was necessary and, finally, confirm that our personal confidence in the lad remained unshaken. It was odds on that the lad had never received a reprimand quite like it before, and the fact that it was originating from someone he respected would hopefully ensure that the reprimand would take effect. This was Rose's theory, anyway, and I can only say that I constantly witnessed the theory turned into successful practice during the time I served with her.

For my part, I never really got out of the beginner's class in the art of reprimanding. I was invariably a slave to my emotions and hopelessly biased in favour of the offender. The lads knew that I was a soft touch. I remember in particular a young lad, Richard, aged 16. He was very small but full of energy and fun, some of which sometimes got misdirected. He had the biggest blue eyes that God ever made and they would sparkle at me beneath his baseball cap, which was about two sizes too large for him. Richard had caused a Saturday night fracas at the roller-skating rink at Milton Keynes and the need for a Monday-morning reprimand arose. I did not relish the prospect. I knew that as soon as he turned those big blue eyes on me from under his oversized baseball cap I would be lost. Sure enough, he did and I was – particularly when he got his apology in first by saying, 'I'm sorry, Smithy, you arrange all these trips for us and I've let you down again, haven't I.' It was much better that the reprimanding be left in the hands of the expert, Rose. I was obviously out of my league.

Such was her supply of energy that no aspect of Rose's duties received less than her full attention. They ranged from shopping and cooking to public relations, from routine administration and maintenance to attendance at courses and meetings, from full involvement in the Friends' activities (I remember her in full voice on the Kop at Liverpool FC) to dealing with her St Matthew's colleagues, and at times and as necessary, the police. But all these activities were, I know, subordinated in her mind to the one essential purpose for which the hostel was built – the care of the young men in her charge. In that, she had a very special quality. She was careful not to have favourites or, more accurately, never to show that she had any favourites. But she did seek out those residents who she felt were perhaps more emotionally damaged than others and who required her special attention. This would be imparted as a special confidence.

I shall always remember two particular cases which were typical of Rose's endeavours in this connection. Edward came to us literally from Northampton Racecourse, where he had been sleeping rough for over a year. During that time he had led a life of almost complete isolation – no family, no friends, no work colleagues, no one. When he reached us he was withdrawn, disorientated, inarticulate and unable to relate either to us or to his peers. He was totally lacking in all self-esteem and self-confidence. He wet his bed regularly. There was no question of armour-plated protection by way of macho behaviour for Edward. His defences were completely down. Rose knew that Edward was a special case and, showing extraordinary patience and perseverance, she literally nursed Edward back to something approaching normality. It took her over a year, but by then he was a very different young man and ready for independent living. I cannot imagine what might have become of Edward if he had never come to us, and more importantly had never come under the influence of Rose.

The other case involved a young man called James. James was a big, powerful but rather ungainly lad, aged 17. He was, to put it

117

mildly, very backward at coming forward. It was not that he had no talents, but rather that he had convinced himself that he had none. Here again was a lad totally lacking in self-esteem. I had found this to be the case with his driving lessons. He was a well-above-average pupil, but I had the biggest job trying to convince him of the fact. When he passed his test first time up, I was in no way surprised. He was gobsmacked. Unlike his peers, he was also a model resident, although withdrawn and to that extent a bit of a loner. Certainly there was no sign of the usual armour plating. I (mistakenly) took it that there was probably no need for it and that James was just a nice harmless guy, carrying no baggage from the past. But Rose apparently saw it differently. She knew or sensed that there was more to James than his rather bland exterior showed, and I recall how hard Rose worked to establish a meaningful relationship with this young man so as to know him, understand him and help him the more.

How right she was to sense that James needed help. It all came home to me one Saturday evening when James terrorised the entire hostel. He had apparently spent the evening drinking heavily, but on his own. He had then returned to the hostel, aggressively drunk and had threatened to 'cut up' three of the other residents in the lounge with a broken beer bottle that he brandished along with his threats. There was already a copious flow of blood from his own cut hand. Rose had been summoned from her flat (rather as one pushes a panic button at a time of crisis) and had started to talk to James in exactly the same soft tone of voice that she used when speaking to him about mundane matters throughout the week.

At first, her words seemed to fall on deaf ears. James continued to brandish his broken bottle and continued his threats to cut everyone up. Indeed, it was a measure of his drunkenness and loss of self-control that his threats and the foul and abusive language that accompanied them were directed at Rose as well as the residents. If there had previously been no evidence of past baggage and anger, there certainly was plentiful evidence right there and then as James held the floor, everyone's attention and, not least, the jagged broken bottle in his hand.

In the end, of course, James's drunken bravado collapsed under the weight of Rose's soft-spoken but non-stop mixture of pleadings and admonishments, delivered in true 'sandwich' fashion as she had taught us. Somehow, her remarks began to hit home. They seemed to stick in James's befuddled brain and brought him back to reality. The broken bottle was handed over and consigned to the dustbin, the damaged hand was bound, and a very distressed but humble James eventually consigned to bed. Rose's performance was brave, sensible and thoroughly professional, but above all it had been fired by a true compassion for a very troubled and vulnerable young man.[5] The incident also taught me that whereas you can bury anger and baggage from the past, you cannot destroy it.

When Rose departed for the YMCA after her long stint with us, we wished her well and feared the worst. We were, of course, delighted for her on her personal promotion and for those resident at the YMCA who were going to benefit from her stewardship there. It was a much bigger hostel than Junction Road with bigger problems and many more problem-makers. But we had no fear that Rose would not do for the YMCA what she had already done for Junction Road. And, of course, she did do it. But where did that leave us? To say that Rose was going to be a difficult act to follow is seriously to understate the case. Our feeling was that she would be an impossible act to follow.

Sure enough, there were then a series of spluttering false starts by way of management appointments, in which, as if to prove our misgivings true, conspicuous square pegs were hammered into equally conspicuous round holes. This interim period of false starts was unsettling, and the Friends were obliged to place their activities on temporary hold. Much more important was the effect it had upon the residents. Although they would never put it in so many words, they had lost the mother figure they revered, and they were in no way enamoured of the nominated replacements. Eventually, a mother figure did appear who proved to be a natural and worthy successor to Rose. It took some time to identify her because, when she first came to us, she was disguised as a cook/housekeeper initially appointed to assist one of the square pegs being hammered into the round hole. It took six months before her true potential was realised and she was handed the full reins.

Her name was Georgina (we called her 'Georgie') Doe and she

---

[5] When I asked her if she had been afraid during the confrontation, Rose replied that she had been more concerned about the blood dripping onto the lounge carpet from James's damaged hand.

came from that delightful border county of Shropshire. In many ways, she reminded us of Rose. She was small in stature and big in personality. She was full of energy and always 'on the go' with plenty to do. But, unlike Rose, she had no previous experience of working in a hostel or any formal training in the care of youngsters (apart from her own two children, who were now grown to adulthood). Her own personal history was linked with hotel management, and we soon found that she was a stickler for cleanliness and tidiness around the hostel – 'Cleanliness is next to godliness' was one of her favourite quotations. We also found out that she was a keen and expert gardener. When on her promotion to the position of hostel manager she inherited the manager's flat at the rear of the premises, she transformed the attached garden into a private haven that must have seemed miles away from the high jinks and noise which normally prevailed in the communal areas of the hostel. But, above all, she was a keen and expert cook, and it was as a result of her culinary skills that she began to make early progress in establishing her own relationship with the lads. She brought to their dining table some of the traditional dishes from her native county. Apart from more than satisfying the requirements of a balanced diet, they also provided the residents with a series of interesting and varied meals that were both appetising and substantial. Our young men had never been fed so well. They appreciated the food – and they soon began to appreciate the cook. For her part, she found it easy to reciprocate. She was a cheerful, uninhibited and generous soul, and it was easy to see even in her early days that her interest in the well-being of the residents went far beyond the sausages she was grilling for their evening meal.

Nevertheless, it was a brave decision by St Matthew's to elevate Georgie to the post of hostel manager. Apart from her professional competence in the kitchen and around the hostel (and in the garden), they were backing their judgement on the basis that the right sort of relationship between her and the lads was both real and clear for all to see, a factor which had been lacking with those others who had followed Rose. The risk was that she would be brought down by her lack of experience and formal training. But if Georgie's appointment proved anything, it was that if the relationship was right with the lads then everything else would fall into place. Mistakes would be made, and were, but the more that Georgie became aware of each lad's personal history and the emotional problems that arose therefrom, the stronger became her feelings of compassion and her resolve to help.

Georgie's emotions were always very close to the surface, and to discover the truth of these young men's lives and be placed in a position to bring them real hope, help and encouragement pulled powerfully on those emotions. She fully admitted that whereas she could cope comfortably with the physical and mental demands of the job (although the completion of the weekly financial returns caused her some dizziness), it was the emotional demands from the residents that sent her stumbling into bed exhausted at the end of the day. She encouraged the lads to bring their problems to her and they took her at her word. It was good evidence that the relationship was working, but Georgie soon found that she was a mother to seven or eight teenage sons, all of whom, for one reason or another, had emotional problems.

Of course, because of her inexperience, she made mistakes. She would reprimand a lad in front of his peers (a cardinal sin). She would be shouting at a lad one minute and giving him a big cuddle the next. She would have favourites and show it (but she changed them on an almost weekly, shift basis). She was inconsistent with her praises, reprimands and punishments leaving the lads confused and sometimes near despair, and she was inconsistent with some of her rulings. She would bring in a new house rule one week and cancel it the next. But in the end these proved to be minor blemishes, because Georgie had the supreme quality of being able to project an overall climate of care and compassion that was picked up by all the lads, recognised by them as the genuine article and to which they responded with an intense personal loyalty.

One of the ways in which she expressed that all-embracing care and love for the community she served was in organising appropriate celebrations to mark a lad's birthday or some other special occasion. Georgie was nothing if not a social bird and she had a real flair for partying and all the razzmatazz that goes with it – and, of course, the lads loved it. I used to think that Georgie invented birthday dates so that we could have a party. But there is no doubt that the fusion of the Friends' cash and Georgie's parties was one of the happiest ways in which we were enabled to add some spice to the young lives in our care. My abiding memory, which pulls all these thoughts together, is the early-morning release of young Michael Daly from the side door of the prison near Henley, where he was greeted by Georgie and me in the drizzle of a very cold early morning. I held the umbrella while Georgie embraced Michael. It seemed that the embrace summed up everything that our hostel was about and why Georgie was such a worthy part of it. The lads knew quite simply that with warts or no warts Georgie loved them and would do everything she could to help them. That was the most priceless gift that could be given them and they knew that. Georgie came as a cook. She stayed to become a kingpin. Rose would have been proud of her.

But, as with Rose, all good things come to an end and eventually Georgie returned to her roots in Shropshire. She never admitted being punch-drunk on her departure, but she did acknowledge a degree of exhaustion that she had never experienced in her life before. Her seven teenage sons had taken their toll, but she retired from the battlefield with honour. There followed a period of nearly six months before a replacement appointment was made. No satisfactory applications had been received to fill the vacancy during this interim period, and the hostel had been run by successive relief managers. Although these were existing St Matthew's staff and therefore thoroughly competent, the lack of continuity was of benefit to no one. Because of the difficulty of making long-term plans, there was minimum activity from the Friends. More importantly, in such circumstances the residents became restless and bored and trouble was likely to ensue. Eventually, however, the skies opened up and delivered to us the latest recruit for taking up the reins at Junction Road.

At least Lynne Rogers conformed with the role model that we were all used to at Junction Road. She was again small in stature, full of energy and with a no-nonsense, businesslike personality that augured well for taking command and getting things done. Fortunately, in terms of case management, the new St Matthew's policy of providing a mixed-age community had been introduced during the interim period, so when Lynne took over in May 2002 she could look forward to less than the usual complement of young men. The more mature new residents would, of course, have had a troubled past or emotional difficulties themselves, and would be looking to St Matthew's to provide them with the safe haven and security that they had perhaps lost and the care that they needed. It was going to be interesting to observe how the new mix would work out. Certainly, the more mature residents ought to have brought some measure of stability and order to the proceedings. It was then hoped that the youngsters would learn to control their own boisterous lifestyle.[6] Lynne therefore set foot on the Junction Road stage at a moment when things were less likely to be dictated by teenage high jinks than in the past, though possibly instead by problems of a different nature. She would perhaps need to be a master of diplomacy rather than a specialist in teenage culture.

In the event, she proved more than equal to the task. She brought a good deal of common sense into a position which demanded that quality above all others, and she was very good at pouring oil on troubled waters. She also showed no lack of determination in facing up to the problems and getting the job done.[7] That Lynne was a competent and businesslike manager with diplomatic skills that ensured that young and old could be accommodated together without undue friction was therefore soon evident; but she was also to show that she was in no way lacking in those more specialised skills and virtues required to mother the younger generation.[8] I was so pleased to see her fall easily and naturally into the precedents set by Rose and Georgie before her.

One example illustrates the point. One of the residents in her care was a young man in his early twenties called Tony. Tony had not been long released from prison at Woodhill, where he had been serving a sentence for attempted murder.[9] Tony's trouble was the difficulty he had in controlling his violent temper. He was attending recommended counselling and anger-control sessions and he appeared to have settled in well at the hostel. Lynne knew he was a special case with a special problem and treated him accordingly. Tony appreciated Lynne's efforts and showed it by his behaviour, which was little short of exemplary. Unfortunately, as was so often the case with these lads, his steady progress was blown apart by an incident, trivial in itself, that led to a major altercation and physical violence on the hostel stairs.

---

[6] The sort of difficulty that could be envisaged would be caused by the lads' music, which was invariably played at the highest decibel level. One lad suggested that more mature applicants should only be admitted providing they were hard of hearing.

[7] She was hampered in the early days by having no private transport, but the Friends were able to make a car available to her until she acquired her own.

[8] It was not that she was inexperienced in these matters. She had three most beautiful teenage daughters. A mere sighting of them by our younger residents was sufficient to stimulate excitement and discussion for the day.

[9] He had found his girlfriend in a compromising position with his best friend and had taken the law into his own hands.

A dispute arose between Tony and a fellow resident concerning the ownership of a mobile telephone. In modern parlance, Tony completely 'lost it'. He used such abusive language and threatening behaviour, which at one stage spilled over into physical assault, that the other young man (and other residents) were badly frightened. The young man ran into his room and locked himself in, whereupon Tony tried to kick the door down. Tony then left the hostel still using abusive language and on the way out further damaged the hostel premises and Lynne's car. It was not until the police arrived that some semblance of order was restored. Tony was charged and Lynne was obliged to attend at the local magistrates' court and give evidence against him. In accordance with the St Matthew's rules Tony was automatically expelled from the hostel, and normally that would have been the end of the matter and the end of Tony. But that discounted Lynne's faith and her confidence that she could still help Tony along the road to rehabilitation if only she was allowed to do so. It also discounted the fact that once Lynne had an idea in her head it was virtually impossible to dislodge it or to prevent it becoming a reality.

Tony should have gone back to prison and remained under expulsion from St Matthew's. He did neither. Within a matter of weeks he was back at Junction Road and his rehabilitation was continuing. I don't know how many ears Lynne had to bend to achieve this desirable state of affairs, but they must have been important ears. When I heard the news my mind went back to Pip, to Michael, to Mick and to countless other young men that we had perhaps been able to help, and I then carefully slotted in the name of Lynne Rogers alongside Rose's and Georgie's. Lynne was now master of the ship, and it was clear that the vessel was in good hands. She is a worthy successor.

Chapter Eight

An Interlude in the Vale of York

'They are ill discoverers that think there is no land, when they can see nothing but sea.'

Francis Bacon (1605)

Early one Saturday morning in December 2002, I took Michael Daly to visit Ampleforth College in the Vale of York. More accurately, Michael took me. Ampleforth is almost 200 miles from Northampton and my advancing years were such that I was no longer fitted for high-speed motorway driving that would involve a 400-mile round trip in the one day. Michael was therefore my chauffeur. He was, of course, one of my star pupils of earlier years.

The occasion of our visit was my wish to cast a seasoned eye over the performance of one of my grandsons, John, who was in his last year as a pupil at Ampleforth and showing some signs of particular prowess as a prominent member of the 1st XV rugger team. Ampleforth College is an independent Catholic public school with some claim to eminence.[1] There are over 500 pupils between the ages of 13 and 19. All but a few are boys and all but a few are resident at the college. On the Saturday of our visit, the Ampleforth 1st XV would be engaged in battle with their Catholic colleagues but arch-rivals, Stoneyhurst College. My grandson had

---

[1] The college is attached to and has grown out of the Benedictine abbey which was first established in the Vale of York by monks who left France at the height of the religious persecutions there. Distinguished old boys from the college range from the Cardinal of Westminster, Basil Hume, to the England rugby captain, Laurence Dallaglio.

assured me that the needle match would be a bloodbath. He apparently viewed that as an attractive feature of the forthcoming game.

There was, of course, another aspect of our visit which I felt might be intriguing. Michael was 18 at the time of our visit, the same age as many of the Ampleforth young men that he was going to see in action and on the sidelines. It was about the only matching characteristic there was. In all other aspects, their personal histories had made them as different as the proverbial chalk from cheese. Most of all, the Ampleforth youngsters came from wealthy or very wealthy backgrounds rooted in strong conventional family affiliations; they already had under their belts the best possible education that money could buy; they spoke for the most part eloquently and with polish as acquired naturally in conversation with family and friends; and finally, perhaps the dividend arising from these advantages, they enjoyed a surfeit of personal confidence and self-esteem. Michael on the other hand came from a background of poverty rooted in a fragmented, ever-shifting and ill-disciplined family unit, whose education had been patchy, poor and at best part-time, who spoke only the limited language of the teenage subculture as acquired from his peers on the street, and whose personal confidence and self-esteem was fragile and limited because of these deficiencies of his earlier life. I suspected that there would be not so much a clash of cultures and class as a stand-off of cultures and class, the one viewing the other as some being from another world. My own loyalties were thus spreadeagled. I was 'up' for Ampleforth of course, for obvious family reasons, and accordingly I took in the pre-match partisan flavour that, if Ampleforth thrashed Stoneyhurst, untold benefits would accrue for the whole human race. But I also felt a strong, fierce loyalty towards Michael, aware of my position as his friend and protector in what could be a strange new experience for him.

Michael's driving was impeccable. How the pupil overtakes the teacher. My daughter had equipped us well with sandwiches to munch our way up the M1/A1, and we were in Ampleforth village in time for Michael to down a well-earned lunchtime pint at The Swan. We had chatted about many things on the way and it was good to know that there was now no barrier or holding back on our conversation. Thus had the relationship grown since the early days. The one thing I noticed about our journey was the number of times we needed to stop for a pee. Although I was well acquainted with the weakness of my own ageing bladder, I began to wonder about lurking chlamydia in Michael's case. I meant to raise the matter with him and should have done, but I did not.

It was in The Swan that Michael had his first sight of some half a dozen Ampleforth seniors and their friends, male and female – and they of him. I do not know what comment, if any, passed among the Amplefordians about the good-looking young fellow sitting up at the corner of the bar with the old fogey they would surely take to be his grandfather. We were probably marked down as locals; that is, until the Midlands burr floated across the bar. As for Michael, he was fascinated not as I first imagined by the demeanour of the youngsters parading before him – joyful and cheerful and pleasantly noisy – but, as he expressed to me in a whisper, 'by the gear on their backs'. He then reminded me that on his personal budget (and that of his mates also) there was always included as a major 'spend' as and when increased income allowed, at least one item of top-quality clothing in the very latest styling. It was a top priority.[2] Unfortunately, the budget would never quite stretch that far, and Michael and his friends could never raise their shop-window browsing to the point of actual purchase; and now here was any amount of quality gear in this country pub. As he said to me as we left, he would have sold his soul for one of the casual jackets on show. The significance did not escape me. What was normal attire to one young man was likened to ermine robes by the other.

The Swan duly emptied its youthful cargo (and me) into the village street as kick-off time for the big match approached. As we made our way to the College 1st XV pitch, we drove down the steep winding path that led us past the main abbey and college buildings. They stood on the very lip of the valley, which stretched for miles below the straggling village of Ampleforth and which took in all the college playing fields that lay in patterned profusion ahead. The buildings themselves were immense and imposing and already steeped in history, forbidding perhaps to the casual visitor but richly endowed for the committed believer. It was humbling to think that a future cardinal of the Church had first bent his knee in prayer as a young teenager at this very spot. But Cardinal Basil Hume had also been captain of the Ampleforth 1st XV before he

---

[2] A peacock must have its feathers.

started on his journey to Westminster. Surely my grandson and his colleagues could count on the Cardinal's spiritual support on this very day.

Soon we were mixed up with a one-way traffic flow, both pedestrians and vehicles, leading down to the 1st XV pitch: a profusion of players, officials, monks, boys and old boys with their families and friends, and not forgetting a small but already noisy contingent of Stoneyhurst supporters wearing their team colours. As with their Amplefordian counterparts, they were already testing out their vocal cords for the cacophonies which lay ahead that afternoon. On arrival at the field of battle we found both teams in their respective huddles undergoing the modern practice of being 'psyched up'. The touchline support for Ampleforth was already vociferous. It was well orchestrated by more than one cheerleader moving around the perimeter and replicating the 'psyching up' process. It seemed that neither the players nor the supporters would be able to give of their best unless they were first whipped into a mood approaching hysteria. I doubted the effectiveness of this ploy (which was deemed unnecessary 100 years ago when I used to play), but then I am not a modernist in these matters. It seemed by now that the whole college and its residents were now in attendance either on the pitch in the team or thronging the touchline in hysterical support. The latter included several of the monks. Each was clad all in black, of course, together with matching gumboots, and as it had just started to drizzle each had an outsize umbrella which when opened accommodated half a dozen pupils as well as the monk himself. That made him cheerleader for the group.

While Michael confessed that he was gobsmacked by the whole spectacle, I mused that I had of course seen the whole thing so many times before.[3] I could never quite dispel the impression that I was witnessing the activities of a very private, exclusive and self-perpetuating club,[4] and that somehow things were more than a little out of perspective and more than a little out of touch with life as Michael and I knew it. It did not seem to me to be a matter of

---

[3] I have three sons. All were prominent sportsmen and all attended Downside, another Catholic public school of similar eminence.

[4] Apart from Michael and the Stoneyhurst contingent, every person in attendance that afternoon was Ampleforth-connected. Of strangers there were none. A good number of the pupils were the brothers or sons of previous pupils, who were themselves similarly related to former pupils.

any prime consequence who were or who were not the victors in a game of teenage football, but I seemed to be in a minority of one. The sight of monks clad in gumboots and brandishing brollies galloping up and down the touchlines in full voice never failed to irritate me. It did at Downside and it still did at Ampleforth. Maybe it is a Benedictine trait. Or maybe it is just me.

And so the game, or battle, began and if limb was not torn from limb it was not for the want of trying. The pace was fast and furious and I had to remind myself that these youngsters were of an age approaching the summit of their physical fitness. Only an old man of my increasing frailty could fully appreciate their good fortune in that respect. I marvelled at their physical resilience. Crash-tackled and hurled to the ground one minute, they bounced up again like rubber balls and made off at high speed seeking new adventures and bigger and better tackles. It was great stuff to watch. They were well coached, too, and had been for at least five years throughout their school careers. They were therefore all skilled in the basics, and each team had their special 'moves', which they had obviously practised assiduously. Their physical fitness and acquired skills were fusing together and some very good rugger was on show as a result. It was exhilarating to watch the free running in open play and just as intriguing to follow the close-quarter skills at the scrums and mauls demonstrated by youngsters who had barely attained manhood. The standard of football was a complete vindication and indeed, fair reward for all the years spent in serious study of rugby football, for the same reason that the scrum-half may also have reached the same high standard in European history.

As might be expected from boys of such similar backgrounds, the two teams were evenly matched, asking and giving no quarter. The forward exchanges were particularly fierce, and John Smith was up to his neck in it. He was trying hard to get the bloodbath going, and I was glad his mother was not there. She would have stopped the proceedings on more than one occasion as her son kept disappearing under a pile of bodies. But gradually, as we approached half-time, it became apparent that Stoneyhurst had one or two very fast, very strong runners outside the scrum, and the Ampleforth defence was hard-pressed to cope with these potential match-winners. The maxim 'Defence wins modern international matches' applies to more than just international matches, and it certainly applied at

Ampleforth on that rather damp day in December. After an afternoon of what was outstanding football, and in spite of continuous and thunderous support for Ampleforth from the touchlines, Stoneyhurst ran out worthy winners.

My grandson left the field of play like a bear with a sore head, lamenting the missed tackles that had settled the issue. Entirely with prejudice as a proud grandfather, I have to say that young John was fully entitled to voice that criticism, because his own defensive play had been faultless. He must have downed every one of the opposition in turn during the afternoon and when the final whistle went could hardly walk off the park for sheer exhaustion. On the flip side, on two occasions he went very close himself to scoring but was held up only yards from the line. In his own words, 'the Stoneyhurst defence was like a brick wall'. Judging by John's bruised and battered body that seemed to be a fair assessment of the position. Nevertheless, I was proud of his personal performance and told him so. I felt well rewarded.

All these events were, of course, closely followed by Michael as well as myself. We had managed to secure a place for the car near a touchline so that we could watch proceedings from the comfort and warmth of the car. But as more followed many to the perimeter we soon found ourselves screened from our unrestricted view. Fortunately, we too had an umbrella and thus we ventured out to stake our claim on the touchline. It was handy being under the cowl of the umbrella because Michael could pass on to me confidential bits of information, raise his queries and state his views in a whisper if he felt so inclined. He was not new to rugby football. He had been with the Friends on more than one occasion to watch Northampton Saints play in the Premier League but had never had the opportunity of playing the game either at school or anywhere else. He soon became very much involved in the battle royal going on in front of him with much vocal support for my own grandson, which pleased me no end. John was an easily identifiable figure. He was not particularly tall, but chunky, heavily built and very fast from a standing start. I had an instinctive sympathy for anyone who got in his way and suffered the inevitable crash tackle, but his main distinguishing feature was something quite different. For reasons best known to himself he always wore very long shorts which came down almost to his knees. He would have fitted well into the photograph of the Ampleforth 1st XV of 1925. I was also pleased to note that he was a crowd favourite. Whenever he won possession of the ball, the cry went up, 'Come on, Smithy,' and it was good to hear Michael in good voice cheering on the third generation Smithy.

At half-time, my interest was sustained by events off the pitch. While the bruised and battered opposing fifteens trudged off to suck lemons, or whatever it is they suck in this modern age, and to rehash their strategies for the annihilation of the enemy, I returned to the comfort of the car and the warmth of the thermos flask. Not so Michael. He had plans of his own and I was an interested spectator. He remained where he was, brolly aloft and baseball cap at a jaunty angle, but he soon started to nudge gently forward so that he could observe the more clearly and hear the more distinctly the proceedings within the small group of Ampleforth lads who were our immediate neighbours on the touchline. If Michael was curious about his neighbours, so were they about him, as I noted more than one furtive look in his direction. Even if not from outer space, Michael certainly stood out as someone very different from all the other lads present that afternoon. Sporting the only baseball cap on show and dressed, shall I say, rather differently to the elegant young gentlemen of Ampleforth, he was worthy of more than one furtive look. Unfortunately, the intimacies never got beyond the furtive looks. I would have liked to have pushed Michael into the middle of the group that interested him so much and to have started some sort of conversation going in the hope of finding common ground. But, on reflection, would that really have been a practical proposition?

On his return to the car, Michael brought with him plenty of comments and questions. Above all, he wanted to know why his neighbours were all so 'posh-looking' and why they spoke so loudly and with such a strange accent using words he did not understand about topics of which he knew nothing. That wasn't too bad as a snap assessment based upon five minutes' observation. I spent the rest of the half-time interval trying to answer his questions. It was very difficult. It was like trying to explain why a German speaks German and a Frenchman speaks French. They were each brought up differently to speak differently, and because of that it was difficult if not impossible for the one to converse with the other or to understand the other. On reflection, I could not help but think that my attempted explanation had expressed a depressing truth.

131

But Michael's most penetrating remark came at the end of the game, when the final whistle called a halt to the proceedings. In accordance with the normal custom which applies in the public schools' rugby system, each team lined up in turn to applaud the opposing team off the field of play. This is to signify, and does, that whereas hard knocks may be taken and given in the most physical of contests, that in no way disturbs the overall spirit of sportsmanship with which the game is played.[5] After watching for the first time what must have seemed a strange procedure to him, Michael floored me with the next question. 'Why is it that after John and his mates have knocked the shit out of each other at Ampleforth on Saturday afternoon, they all line up and applaud one another off the pitch, but when I and my mates knock the shit out of each other in Abington Street[6] on Saturday evening, we're all rounded up and put in police vans to appear before the magistrates on Monday morning?' I hesitated to pile on the agony by informing him that the magistrates that he and his friends would face on the Monday morning were likely to be the sort of gentry who would have been educated at Ampleforth and the like and whose ability to understand and communicate with the likes of Michael and his friends was therefore almost certainly next to nil.

It was not a very positive thought with which to end the afternoon, but it chimed in well with my own grandson's long and uninterrupted harangue about Ampleforth's defensive inadequacies as we joined him and the somewhat bedraggled Amplefordians making their way back to college and the hot showers, crumpets and tea that awaited them. Flaws in the judicial system and Ampleforth's defensive inadequacies. The world was full of problems.

As we said our farewells to John, who was still banging on about the defensive frailties of his teammates, we again passed alongside the foreboding structure of the abbey buildings. On an instinct, I stopped the car and suggested to Michael that we pay a visit just for a few moments to what was, after all, one of the most important shrines in the country commemorating the great saint who founded the Benedictine order. The abbey had already spawned one cardinal of the Church in Basil Hume of Westminster. Maybe Michael would experience a Damascene conversion and follow in the footsteps of

---

[5] It used to be said that a game of rugger would sweat the vice and anger out of you.
[6] A street in Northampton.

132

the cardinal on the road to Westminster, the red hat and papal glory. Maybe that or maybe something more simple.

I remember Michael telling me that when he was at Yarmouth for a weekend holiday, he enjoyed most of all just sitting on the beach in the evening twilight when all the holidaymakers had disappeared and he was alone with the vastness of the sea stretched out before him, and the only sound was the gentle breaking of the waves on the seashore. Although he knew he was alone, he said that he had no feeling of loneliness but rather, as he put it, one of 'belonging'. He was not afraid, although he sometimes sat until it was quite dark. I remember how impressed I had been with Michael's experience and his description of it. It seemed that he had stumbled upon the essential truth of man's perspective and his humility before the works of nature. I wondered if he might experience that same sense of perspective and humility inside the Benedictine abbey. As we entered, I told him to take a seat anywhere among the rows of pews that stretched out in front of him and then to take in the silence that surrounded him. He might then experience that same sense of loneliness and yet communion that he had had at the seaside. I then positioned myself at some distance from Michael and spent my time storming heaven and, in particular, the great Saint Benedict with my personal prayers for Michael and all those homeless and underprivileged young men like him. I rose to join Michael as we made our exit. I did not mention or discuss with him any conclusions from our few minutes with Saint Benedict. We resumed our seats in the car and turned southwards as the gloom and mists came rolling in across the valley.

On our way home, Michael asked lots more about all that he had seen and heard that afternoon. He was clearly mystified as to why anyone should have to travel nearly 200 miles simply to go to school. In his experience, school was just around the corner or thereabouts, and certainly within walking distance. When I explained that Ampleforth was not part of the state system of education and school fees there had to be paid over and above what I had already paid as my contribution to the state system through general taxation, he was even more mystified. When I told him that what I was doing for John was only the same as that which I had already done for each of my own four children, he expressed his near incredulity with the obvious question as to why. It was a short question that required a long answer and I took the best part of the journey

133

home trying to supply it. I am sure that Michael was convinced by part of my reasoning and I am pleased to see that at least he was having a good think about the rest of it. He could readily understand the advantages that flowed at Ampleforth, from the low teacher–pupil ratio, which virtually guaranteed personal tuition for each pupil with the academic subjects, to the profusion of extra classroom activities I had described to him, which meant if a lad had a talent, whether it be playing rugger, the violin or the fool on a stage, then it would be developed and brought to fruition. He could readily appreciate the advantages of communion and the development of community spirit (of which the afternoon's activities had been a good example). Michael not only understood and appreciated these things; he made it clear that he was also deeply envious of those who enjoyed them. But, as I explained to him, these advantages, important as they were, could be obtained at other educational establishments closer to Northampton than the Vale of York, among them some of the best schools within the state system. So I explained that it was in fact another factor which took John nearly 200 miles to school and it was this factor that I spent so much time discussing on our way home.

I told him that my wife and I had nurtured our four children through their early lives to believe certain things about the purpose of their existence and the values they should seek in living their lives. Those beliefs and values were those of a Christian tradition going back some 2,000 years, as expressed in the articles of faith and moral teaching of the Catholic Church. Unfortunately, present-day Britain was no longer a Christian country but a secular state governed by those with secular views. These views, which were so different from those of Christian origin were, as one might expect, propagated vigorously through government policies and extensive media coverage, through television, radio and press. Not least, these views were also propagated through the state education system. Under those unfortunate circumstances, my wife and I had decided that we should do everything possible to protect the traditional Christian faith of our children from exposure to the standards and values so apparent in present-day Britain, which we considered deplorable. We therefore resolved to sustain and protect the home influence with a school influence running in parallel, that is, a school which propagated Christian philosophy and Christian values. That is what had led us to seek out the great Benedictine

134

establishments of Downside, where my three sons were educated, and now Ampleforth, where a grandson was in his last year. It had, of course, led inevitably to considerable financial stringency over many years, but, as I confirmed to Michael, it had been well worth it. That is why the policy had been continued into the second generation and that was why we were travelling 400 miles that day to visit young John at his school. At Downside and now at Ampleforth, we had found regimes[7] which mirrored precisely the beliefs and values that we had nurtured in the early days and which my children and grandchildren continue to nurture to this day. In place of the secular philosophy of 'the freedom of the individual', which seems to have promoted a climate of selfishness and materialism in present-day Britain, we found educational establishments that placed personal responsibility ahead of personal rights, self-control ahead of control of others, humility ahead of naked ambition and honesty ahead of expediency. At least we had felt that we were aiming at the right target, even though our own personal efforts might have been off tack from time to time. In this regard, my less than perfect exposition might just have left Michael curious and wanting to know more.

And so we were soon rolling down Abington Street in the middle of Northampton with not a police van in sight. It had been an interesting day and I am sure that Michael enjoyed it as much as I did.

---

[7] On one famous occasion, the headmaster of Downside (or was it Ampleforth?) was asked what he considered was the most important factor in preparing his pupils for life, to which he replied, 'We do not prepare our pupils for life. We prepare them for their death.' The religious significance of this reply may be lost on a non-believer.

Chapter Nine

Been There ... Done That

'*A great devotee of the Gospel of Getting On.*'
George Bernard Shaw (1898)

At the end of 2002, after one or two false starts, I finally retired from my position with the Friends of Valerie Hanson House. I was 77 years old by then. Although the spirit was still willing the body was beginning to rebel and fall apart.[1] In addition, the new policy at the hostel of mixing the young with the old did not excite me, although I understand the reasons why St Matthew's made the change. Fortunately, my retirement did not entirely sever my connection either with the hostel or with the young men it had served. I still visit Lynne, battling bravely on at Junction Road, and I also visit some of the 'old boys' now living independently (mostly with their lady loves). I am therefore kept reasonably up to date with all the news.

So what did I learn during the ten years or so that I was in the saddle? What conclusions can be fairly drawn from the experience? In particular, what are the problems posed both to society and to themselves by our young men, bearing in mind that there are an estimated 100,000 other homeless youngsters like them in modern-day Britain. And how and why do these problems arise and what remedies can be suggested to correct the position? I think I made it

---

[1] One of my Christmas presents was a walking stick from my daughter. Arthritis, which had lurked for years around my fingers and wrists, had at last taken serious hold. My heart was also threatening to jump off its hook.

clear in the early chapters that when I was first drawn into active participation for the welfare of our first residents, it was with a combination of curiosity and ignorance as well as genuine compassion. It was rather like reaching for a new book from the library shelf. The title sounded interesting enough, but a quick browse through only confirmed my ignorance of the subject matter. A detailed study of the book, probably over an extended period, would be necessary before a full understanding could be obtained, curiosity satisfied and conclusions drawn. And so with my adventures at Junction Road.

The problems posed to society by our young men are not difficult to identify. They are rooted in the very nature of the lads themselves. Well on the way to adulthood by the time they reached us, our youngsters were largely incapable of and in some cases even unwilling to take their place as responsible citizens in the general community. That is because they were for the most part desperately undereducated (some were almost illiterate) and they had developed no particular vocational skills that they could sell in the labour market. They were therefore virtually unemployable. There was another common factor which adversely affected their attractiveness both in terms of employment and acceptance into the general community. Because of what can only be described as their unfortunate backgrounds and personal histories they were in the generality emotionally immature and subject to erratic and sometimes aggressive behaviour. It was because of these deficiencies that our young men were almost bound to become a burden on society rather than a boost to it.[2]

One of the biggest specific problems posed to society as a manifestation of the above difficulties was the financial burden of supporting these young men, who were incapable of supporting themselves. The burden was of course borne by the general body of taxpayers, although the administration was handled by the Department of Social Services.[3] These costs were enormous. They included not only maintenance payments while the lads were unemployed,[4] but also the costs of a whole industry which has

---

[2] There were, of course, exceptions but only so many as to prove the general rule.

[3] I was never able to entirely convince our youngsters that the fortnightly giro cheque from the DSS (upon which their financial life depended) was a handout from those taxpayers who were working and was in no way an 'entitlement'.

[4] These payments were made under various labels ('Young Person's Allowance', 'Job Seeker's Allowance', 'Housing Benefit', etc., etc.) according to the latest political initiative or soundbite of the Government of the day. Different labels or not they all amounted to the same thing which was unemployment pay.

grown up in an attempt to reintroduce these young people to mainstream living and keep them away from the street and out of the police courts. An army of social workers, youth counsellors, probation officers, job-centre advisers, youth-offender teams, drug- and alcohol-addiction advisers, anger-control groups, victim-support agencies, etc., etc. all exist (and thrive) for this purpose. And like all bureaucracies these agencies grow and grow like topsy and the taxpayer picks up the tab. The costs on a national scale must be astronomical.

There was another cost to society, or more accurately what amounted to a serious wastage of what should have been an integral part of the nation's resources. It was an item that constantly nagged at me whenever I glimpsed the inherent intelligence of some of the lads so often hidden behind their protective shields of macho behaviour. I thought of all the potential skills in these young men lying fallow and undeveloped because of earlier neglected education and vocational training, and how that was so much to the nation's disadvantage. So many of our lads were obliged to opt eventually for posts of employment way below their natural intelligence but in line with their restricted education.[5] Three examples spring readily to mind of young men of rare intelligence. If the young men in question had been my own sons they would have benefited from a good education. Such was their intelligence, I am sure that they would have then been worthy of entering a major university and subsequently qualifying in a learned profession or other skilled vocation with benefit to themselves but also to the nation as a whole. In fact, of the three young men I have in mind, one drives a van, another is a junior clerk and the third is an unemployed drug addict. That is a shameful waste of the nation's resources. There are 100,000 homeless young men in Britain. Not all are of exceptional intelligence, but based upon our experience at Junction Road, a good proportion most certainly are.

A third problem for society also engaged our attention at Junction Road. It was potential rather than actual, but serious in its implications. Sooner or later, our residents had to face up to a decision. Either they were going to cooperate fully with our attempts to get them off the streets, away from the police courts and into full-time

---

[5] With the odd exception, none of our residents could produce School Leaving Certificates of any great worth in terms of academic results. That was because their attendance at school had been spasmodic at best and non-existent at worst.

employment or courses of study, or they were not. They were truly at a crossroads in their young lives. It was the consequences of making the wrong decision both for the individual and society generally that worried me. Of course, to the outsider the making of the right decision and its implementation were simple matters of common sense, but my experience at Junction Road told me that neither was the case. Readers of the earlier pages will realise that there was a common thread which seemed to link all our residents. There were of course exceptions but in the main their case histories revealed much-troubled backgrounds, including varying degrees of neglect, isolation, rejection and even abuse, either mental, physical or sexual. Their educational attainments were usually severely substandard and little seems to have been done to instil in them any sense of self-discipline or meaningful social intercourse other than with their own associates. As a result of these adverse factors, all rooted in their pasts, they were emotionally insecure, subject to irrational behaviour and possessed of severe hang-ups relating to the Establishment in general and those whom they blamed for their misfortunes in particular (one or more parents, other family members, step-relatives, teachers, social workers, etc.). Thus, a lot of them had opted out of mainstream living and found for themselves a cosy corner in a street culture which was answerable to no one but the users themselves. None of the Establishment rules and regulations applied. As a result, the street was the natural habitat of our young men not a place on the mainstream bandwagon. And we were now asking our young men to relinquish their cosy corner on the street, where no one bothered them, and step back into a system which at least in their view had already kicked them in the teeth and humiliated and rejected them. It was not an easy decision for our young men to make.

Our lovable rogue, Michael Daly,[6] after more than one stab at it, made the right decision and then made himself physically ill trying to implement the decision by taking up regular employment. To his eternal credit, he battled on and made it in the end. He is now firmly strapped to the mainstream bandwagon. Our Mick the Lad, Michael Crague,[7] made the wrong decision initially and ended up in Woodhill Prison. But it was Mick's subsequent explanation

---

[6] See Chapters Six and Eight.
[7] See Chapter Four.

to me that was so disturbing. It made me realise just how such a wrong decision could be made and the problems that could arise in consequence.

Mick had found things tough after his release from Glen Parva Young Offenders Unit. With our help he had tried hard to join the mainstream. He had applied for a job with his old employer, B&Q, and others, but all had rejected his applications (according to Mick, because of 'Establishment' rules). As a result Mick had no job and no money. But his friends had money. So Mick went back to his street activity, which was burglary. That gave him money (and a prison sentence).

Here was the problem for society. One hesitates to suggest that B&Q and others get the burglars they deserve. But the fact is that the likes of our young men, with warts and all (and there were many), must be so enabled to make their way in 'our' world that they will not hesitate to make the right decision about their future. Our young men were always teetering on the edge of criminal activity as an alternative to mainstream living. Although we certainly had some notable successes in heading off such unwelcome proclivities, I often wondered if any of our your men would eventually slide into full-time criminal activity still driven by that old inner anger directed against the Establishment and rooted in an unfortunate past. As the abused becomes the abuser, so the deprived becomes the thief. That was the first part of the story of our Mick the Lad and thousands like him. Fortunately, in his case, the help was sustained and he won through in the end. And the others?

There was a further problem, a big one, which had to be borne not by society but by the young men themselves. I was once asked by a leading intellectual, 'Haven't you got anything better to do with your time than look after life's losers?' I was not shocked. It was the sort of question I might expect from a present-day, fully paid-up devotee of the 'Doctrine of Getting On'. He had certainly got on. He was a professor at a leading British university. Our lads had definitely not got on. They were for the most part unemployed and unemployable. As far as he was concerned, the labels were correctly attached and that was the end of the matter. He was a winner. Our lads were self-evident losers. I ought to have been a winner but was not because, according to him, I was wasting my time in a useless activity. I tried to explain to our egghead friend that if life was a race, as he seemed to be implying, then whereas he and I were starting that race way down the track by reason of our parentage, stable backgrounds and education, our lads, bereft of all these advantages, were starting it way behind the start line and each carrying heavy baggage from an unfortunate past. In these circumstances, should not the winners turn back and help the losers? The only reaction I got was a shrug of the shoulders. Compassion was no part of winning.[8]

The personal problem that had to be faced by our young men was therefore twofold. Their race, or rather their way through life, was by reason of their background and history bound to be difficult, frustrating and desperately unfair, at least in terms of the search for earnings, possessions and all the other trappings of the material world. Furthermore, in a land which seems to be in the firm grip of the devotees of the 'Doctrine of Getting On', it would appear that those intent upon winning are unlikely to find the time to pause and turn back to help those who are clearly losing.[9] Of course, some of our lads will buck the trend, and good luck to them. They will grind hard and true and their strength of character will carry them through all the difficulties until they end up as winners. But it is not those that concern me. It is the others, weighed down with the burdens of the past and looking in vain for help from the present.

The cause of these problems affecting both society and the lads themselves is as easy to identify as the problems themselves. Our young men had not for the most part reached adulthood when taking up residence with us. Primary responsibility for their maintenance and welfare, their education and emotional development and their guided entry into mainstream living did not therefore rest with the Department of Social Services or with St Matthew's Housing or with us helpers at Junction Road. It rested with their parents. Unfortunately, that responsibility had not, for one reason or another,

---

[8] Or was it? It depends upon which measuring stick is being used.

[9] During my time at Junction Road I was constantly amazed at the ease with which I could raise cash for a special project for the lads and how this contrasted with the difficulties of enlisting hands-on help with the selfsame project. 'Charity without involvement' seemed to be the rule. The same rule appeared to apply even to such an illustrious institution as the Benedictine abbey and college at Ampleforth, where one of my grandsons was educated. There was always the most generous cash support for charitable causes far across the seas in all parts of the world. But a request to use old school buildings fringing the playing fields as part of a much-needed drug rehabilitation centre was booted firmly into touch. A priest friend of mine once told me, 'Dirty hands are the sign of true compassion.'

been discharged. In every case, our young men were the products of what have become known as 'broken' homes[10] and the defective parenting that was spawned by that unhappy circumstance.

The collapse of responsible parenting has been a strong feature of post-1970s Britain, and has been accompanied and encouraged by the parallel increase in the number of broken homes. Unfortunately, it was into this unstable and fluid social environment that the majority of our young men had been born. The period in question has been described as 'the age of the sexual revolution' and 'the era of sexual emancipation'. Nevertheless, it had been hoped that attaching these modern and fashionable labels to what is, after all, a rather ancient activity had not blinkered the participants to the obvious point that indulgence in sexual activity carries with it the obligation to face up to the responsibilities that may ensue from such activity, which might well include responsibility for the procreation of a new life.

Of course, in the sophisticated world in which we live that latter eventuality should never be the case unless so required. Contraceptives and abortions are now universally available to avoid the consequences while retaining the pleasures of the activity.[11] Nevertheless, our young men, avoiding all such preventative hazards, duly arrived safely from the womb and, in accordance with what must surely be the most natural law of life itself, were then entitled to look for that unique love and protection and all those other benefits that should flow from parents who understand their responsibilities and are anxious to discharge them. That was always the birthright of every newborn baby. Hopefully, it still is. It is founded on the observation born of experience that the unselfish and painstaking investment of time thus spent by both parents does, in ultimate terms, produce children well able to make their way in the world as rounded, emotionally secure and confident young people.

It is not denied that the required investment of time, energy and money[12] by dutiful parents is both long-term and arduous. Their

---

[10] A broken home is defined here as a home, originally established on a permanent basis by man and wife or cohabiting couple, where one of the parties has subsequently deserted the other party (and any children) and left the home. The home has been 'broken' by reason of that person's departure.

[11] Unfortunately, however, the resulting promiscuity has led to significant increases in the incidence of sexually transmitted diseases and other problems.

[12] My own dear mother once told me, 'You can have children or you can have money, but you cannot have both.'

142

responsibilities are many and various. In the very early days, they need to concentrate on the creation of a happy and stable home and the constant expression of love, care and protection for the infant child. Later on, there follows the active nurturing of the growing youngster through all the stages of his development. This includes arranging, encouraging and helping with his education, advising on behavioural problems, helping with character formation, instilling self-discipline, encouraging intellectual, cultural and sporting interests, giving moral guidance and, not least, acting as an honest-to-goodness friend and confidant encouraging easy and open communication. These responsibilities need to be given the highest priority in the home by both parents, but then the prize is beyond value.

It need hardly be said that these unique and invaluable gifts of responsible parenting cannot be dispensed by the Department of Social Services or by the St Matthew's Society or by the volunteers at Junction Road. They can only be provided by loving parents intent upon discharging their proper responsibilities. Unfortunately, our young men had seemingly never tasted these fruits. In almost every case, they were living witnesses to parental neglect of varying degrees,[13] which arose directly from the circumstance of a broken home.

Immediately following such a breakup, in practical terms day-to-day caring for any children of the broken union becomes the responsibility of one parent only. We then have a single person trying to cope with a two-handed job. That is, until such time as the inevitable stepmother/father puts in an appearance to create divided loyalties and a stranger-in-blood relationship between a so-called parent (stepfather/stepmother) and the child.[14] This unhappy state of affairs (at least as far as the children are concerned) was the direct cause in so many cases of our youngsters leaving home. These breakups seem almost preordained among young people when they first form relationships and start cohabiting. The relationship is based upon some sort of 'permanent maybe' arrangement on the understanding that if 'things don't work out', the relationship can be ended and further fields and pastures new explored.[15] This

---

[13] Rose Stewart described them as 'blooms that were never allowed to blossom' and 'buds that were never opened and ripened.'

[14] So typical of the case histories of our young men and the sort of circumstances (where a stepfather replaces the natural father of a daughter) which have led to charges of sexual abuse.

[15] One gets the impression with some of these cohabiting arrangements that either or both parties are 'halfway out of the door with their hat on' from the day that the cohabiting starts. Or perhaps it's from the day when the sexual glamour starts to fade.

absence of any long-term commitment, the lack of permanence and the inherent instability of the arrangement are all factors easily picked up by young children as and when they arrive, and the eventual ending of the relationship between the parents can be devastating to a youngster's emotional stability and self-confidence, torn as he is by a loyalty to both parents. But his emotional needs are very much in second place. It is his parents' sexual needs that seem to top the bill in the present climate.[16]

Unfortunately, and to its immortal shame, society itself appears to have played its part in this neglect insofar as it no longer appears to ascribe the same high priority to responsible parenting within the confines of a stable family home as used to be the case. As a result, the incidence of broken homes has increased dramatically since the 1970s, as has the number of homeless youngsters. To that extent, the present problems constitute self-inflicted wounds. The present secular philosophy, apparently embraced by public opinion, seems to prioritise above all else the right of 'self-expression'. The clarion call of the 1970s, it promotes the message (and massage) of self-expression in all its forms, which in fact appears to encourage little more than the pursuit of material acquisition, personal adornment and lifestyle, wealth accumulation and sexual gratification. The inebriates of that philosophy are therefore hardly likely to listen to a softer, older, wiser and more sober philosophy preaching that true happiness (which must be the aim of every society) can never come from a policy of self-indulgence as a 'devotee of the Gospel of Getting On'. Rather does it arise from the act of giving as an expression of love by one person for another person. And how better can that love be expressed than by the act of self-sacrifice involved in the upbringing of children, the natural fruit of meaningful sexual union? That is a secret of life as yet undiscovered by the modern devotees of the 'today's the day' script.

Unfortunately, present-day Britain appears to be well stocked with devotees of the 'Gospel of Getting On'. If living in accordance with the tenets of that doctrine involves a clash with parental responsibilities or any other selfless act, then it would seem that self-gratification will tend to score over self-sacrifice. Nowhere is this more evident than in the typical broken home. Very little social

---

[16] The circumstances described were related to me by one of our youngsters, who was the victim in such a case. He told me that if he ever met the father who had deserted him, he would kill him. Such was the anger of the lad, aged 17, that I believed him.

stigma now attaches to a man who walks out on his home and family, avoids responsibility for the upkeep and welfare of his own children and seeks (sexual) pastures new. Such behaviour[17] is now almost socially acceptable and is often dismissed with a shrug of the shoulders as 'just one of those things'. It seems that according to modern standards, the right of a man or woman to satisfy their sexual appetites now outweighs any responsibilities that may have arisen from previous sexual activity, including those following in the wake of the procreation of a new life.

The real losers from this sort of reprehensible behaviour are, of course, the innocent children left in limbo without a real mum or dad. I know that this was the case with so many of our lads and I know how deep ran the scars. It is a sad commentary on the standards and values of modern Britain. Anecdotal evidence of this state of affairs is readily available from our experience at Junction Road. During the entire course of my time there I only ever met the fathers of two of our residents. Absence may make the heart grow fonder, but in my experience the prolonged absence of a young man's father was more likely to produce heartbreak and inner anger than any increased fondness. The first father I met shook my hand and told me that people called him God. I don't think that God could have been flattered. The man shaking my hand was small and fat, sported a large beer belly and stank of stale beer. I had never imagined God so. During our conversation, which included his new 'partner' (by way of an irritating adjunct) as well as his son, I noticed that Michael, the lad, aged 16, kept well away from his father, edging his way around the table that stood in the centre of the reception area. After his father and escort had left, I enquired of Michael why he seemed so keen to put clear blue water between him and his father. The answer came back like a shot and was no surprise. 'He used to beat me and I'm still afraid of him.' Some God.

The second occasion when I met a father would have been almost comical if it had not been so shocking. I was approached by the father of a young lad, John, who found himself in the magistrates' court for a minor offence (shoplifting), although he was already on probation. The father wished to sue the Probation Service for

---

[17] A practice euphemistically described as 'falling in love with someone else'. It usually has nothing to do with love and everything to do with sexual gratification.

negligence in that they had failed to keep young John out of trouble. He didn't seem to know or want to know that the person primarily responsible for keeping young John out of trouble was himself. Quite simply, he wanted to sue someone for not discharging his own responsibility. The irony did not register and he got quite agitated when I pointed out where the primary responsibility lay. It was a good example of how the social-services bureaucracy is ingrained into ordinary modern-day living and is used and abused by people to evade personal responsibility. Unfortunately, this had been the case with so many of our young men and their parents.

If the problems presented to society by our youngsters, and their causes, are easily identified, so also is the remedy.[18] The difficulty is how to ensure that the remedy can be applied in the sort of society in which we presently live, which currently subscribes to very different behavioural priorities from those required to effect a remedy. It is certainly clear to me, based upon my experiences over the last ten years, that the problems associated with the growing number of homeless young men will continue and even worsen unless there is a radical rethink of present-day sexual ethics, or the lack of them,[19] coupled with a return to responsible and high-priority parenting set in the stability and permanence of the traditional old-style family unit. This new thinking,[20] and the concomitant behavioural changes, both of which would necessarily include a degree of self-sacrifice and personal restraint, are hardly likely to be received with acclamation either by the populace in general, who are subjected to pressure from media interests, or by those powerful strands in society who have large and lucrative investments directed towards satisfying the imagined needs and wants of the devotees of the 'Doctrine of Getting On'. Above all else, that doctrine is based upon the relentless pursuit of material acquisitions. The attainment of that objective provides the opportunity for lucrative profits and a ready market for those powerful commercial interests

---

[18] I have no doubt that the work done by the St Matthew's Society and the Friends at Junction Road was important and of value, but we all knew that our efforts were directed towards alleviating the effect of the problems rather than attacking their cause.

[19] So beautifully and accurately described in present-day terms by Pip Bailey (see Chapter Two) as 'an extension of the entertainments industry for which you do not have to pay'.

[20] It is of course better described as a return to 'old' thinking which has been the case for over 2,000 years. Retracing one's steps is not necessarily retrograde. It can be considered as the retracing of one's steps along a road leading nowhere to rejoin the main thoroughfare leading everywhere.

which dominate life in present-day Britain. The thinking goes, if the collateral damage in the race for profits and personal enhancement includes broken homes, hurt kids and the creation of more of life's losers on the way, then so be it. At least the harvest of profits has been safely gathered, which appears to be the main priority.

The difficulty presented by an entrenched thought process conditioned to materialism and encouraged by a secular philosophy should not be underestimated. At present, every public body – from Parliament to the BBC and other TV companies, to the newspapers – rides high on the secular bandwagon, which faces in the opposite direction to that required. As a result, public opinion today is overwhelmingly secular in its beliefs and behavioural priorities. Shorn of all niceties, those beliefs and priorities amount to satisfying every personal indulgence and very little else. It is a society where aspirations seldom rise higher than the need to do well in the marketplace and the date of the next promotional sale. Selfishness prevails over selflessness, and in commercial terms the projection and maintenance of this naked materialism (under the guise of 'self-expression') is relentless. A powerful advertising industry promises us instant pleasure and happiness every minute of every day providing we buy either this or that item without delay. The TV advertisements themselves are often unintelligible but are invariably enlivened and lubricated by generous helpings of sexual titillation. They exhort us to buy things that we do not need and cannot afford other than by piling more debt upon an ever-increasing mountain of personal credit.[21] Such is the frenzied exploitation of self-expression in the marketplace. It is self-expression through self-indulgence. Responsible parenting is an example of the opposite. That is self-expression through self-sacrifice. The problem of how to bring about the required change in attitude is indeed immense.

The present-day frenzy associated with the commercial exploitation of the imagined material needs and wants of the public is not the only problem that has to be faced in attempts to produce the sort of social climate which might be sympathetic to the required new thinking. It is matched by the frenzy associated with the perceived need of the young and the not so young to maintain high levels of

---

[21] I have often wondered if one or more of the (untrue) sale 'puffs' included on display cards and in TV advertising could be elevated to a condition of sale and the vendor sued for fraudulent misrepresentation. Perhaps some day an enterprising lawyer will take this matter up.

personal sexual excitement and experience. As a result, sexual promiscuity in this country has reached epidemic proportions.[22] Of course, the media interests, including the cinemas and live theatres as well as TV, radio, newspapers and the publishing industry, generally all know that nothing sells like sex. The presentation of sex in all its forms is the biggest and most profitable industry in the world today and the media, certainly not discouraged by the government of the day, have therefore long carried the message that sex must also be the most important thing in the world. The present scale of promiscuous behaviour would appear to indicate that at least in this country the message has been received and understood and the bait well and truly taken. After all, sexual gratification is yet another mode of self-expression or so the modernists would have us believe. Yet again, the difficulty in securing the required changes in attitudes and the resurrection of some sort of sexual ethic should not be underestimated. There is no doubt that the greatest single cause of today's broken homes, which spawn so many of our homeless youngsters, is the sexual infidelity of one parent or the other or both. But there is also no doubt that any call to renounce this sort of sexual debasement and instil some semblance of ethical law and order on this front will be vigorously opposed by those presently intoxicated by their absence.

An examination of all these modern-day appetites, pressures and priorities leading to the breakup of relationships and the promotion of an environment manifestly unsuitable to the cause of responsible parenting indicates clearly those factors which need promoting to bring about the opposite effect. All these factors stand or fall on the essential ingredients of self-sacrifice and self-restraint. These ingredients need to replace the present self-indulgence, which demeans and disfigures present-day Britain. All great civilisations were built and sustained by the rule of law based upon self-control and self-restraint.[23] That is to say, 'personal expression' by way of

---

[22] As have the unfortunate by-products by way of record levels of abortions, unwanted pregnancies, single-parent families, marital breakdowns, broken homes, broken hearts, rapes, sexual offences against minors, and the highest incidence yet in sexually transmitted diseases including infection with the HIV virus, syphilis, gonorrhoea, chlamydia and thrush.

[23] In those areas of the world where the rule of law does not run and the need for self-control and self-restraint is unrecognised, the most appalling fratricide has occurred, involving the death of millions. Central Africa during the late twentieth century has been a case in point. The incidence of infection from the HIV virus is another example from that unhappy continent.

148

undue self-indulgence and self-gratification is consciously reined in for the benefit of the community at large. Precisely the same principle would apply in a civilised homestead. The bonding mechanism or rule of law in the homestead would be the mutual love existing between the two cohabitees and the children. As far as the growing children are concerned, the time period for this love bonding would be forever. Death is not an item admitted to a child's mind. As far as the cohabitees are concerned, there would be no escape from the bonding to each other. That is because there would be a solemn undertaking between the parties in the first place. They would therefore both have to be very very careful in choosing their lifetime mate, and there would have to be more to it than sexual attraction alone.[24] Only when death intervened would the arrangement come to an end. There is a word for such an arrangement. It is called marriage. Sexual activity could then take its proper, predestined place in the arrangement, becoming the physical expression of the love bonding between man and wife. No longer would it be the mechanical act of a mindless culture. Nor would it be an extension of the entertainment industry. It would become instead the personal, private, intimate, meaningful and ordained physical expression of the love of each party in the marriage for the other, and a gift reserved for that other person and that person alone. If a new life is procreated in such circumstances, it will have been so created out of love and with love. Is there any doubt that the new life would be the subject of responsible parenting and a constant mirror of its parents' love for each other?

Of course, devotees of the 'Doctrine of Getting On' will say that the suggested arrangements, which have served mankind for the best part of 2,000 years, are 'not practical'. Of course that is true, but only as between the said devotees. After all, they already have their own commitment, which is to themselves alone. There can therefore be no case for sustained living with others in a communal homestead and the forsaking of personal material needs and wants, including sexual gratification, for the sake of the homestead community. That indeed would be an absurdly theoretical proposition. But somewhere, somehow, there may be, as the Bard himself has said, 'a light that shines in this naughty and dark world' where

---

[24] Common sense would look for a period of friendship deepening into intimacy and based upon mutual respect as an essential preliminary.

decent men and women will lift their eyes and aspire to all that is good but difficult, rather than trundling on with all that is bad because it is easy. It is inconceivable to me that this great country of ours should have fallen off the moral tramlines in the manner that it has. My experience and adventures at Junction Road brought home to me the extent and effect of parental neglect, the hurt inflicted on the innocent and decent youngsters I was privileged to meet and know and, perhaps worst of all, the apparent indifference to their plight from those more fortunately placed. Charitable Christmas giving is one thing;[25] eradication of the cause of distress is quite another. That requires a drastic rethink particularly by all those inebriated devotees of the 'Doctrine of Getting On'. It also requires a fundamental moral reawakening. That may just please a hitherto-unknown silent majority who have perhaps had enough of the bombastic but shallow chatter from the secular world. Let us hope so, anyway.

---

[25] Do the donors know that the distressing circumstances which bring their charitable feelings to the fore in the Christmas month of December are still the case for the other eleven months of the year?

Postscript

At 3.40 a.m. on Sunday 28 March 2004, a motor vehicle stood at the top of a hill just outside Northampton. There were no lights, but the engine was running and there was a hosepipe connecting the exhaust to the car interior. There was a sole occupant. He was one of those young men mentioned in this book. Before the carbon monoxide could take full effect, a police patrol vehicle arrived. The young man was taken to the local mental hospital. After examination and assessment he discharged himself voluntarily the next day.